STF ... JESS

SELF-PROMOTION SECRETS FOR MUSICIANS

Michael Gelfand

SCHIRMER
TRADE
BOOKS

A Part of **The Music Sales Gr...**
New York/London/Paris/Sydney/Copenhagen/B...

D1418863

Schirmer Trade Books
A Division of Music Sales Corporation, New York

Exclusive Distributors:
Music Sales Corporation
257 Park Avenue South, New York, NY 10010 USA

Music Sales Limited
8/9 Frith Street, London W1D 3JB England

Music Sales Pty. Limited
120 Rothschild Street, Rosebery, Sydney, NSW 2018, Australia

Order No. SCH 10144
International Standard Book Number: 0.8256.7304.6

Printed in the United States of America

Cover Design: Josh Labouve

Library of Congress Cataloging-in-Publication Data

Gelfand, Michael, 1966-
  Strategies for success: self-promotion secrets for musicians / by Michael Gelfand.
     p. cm.
  ISBN 0-8256-7304-6 (pbk. : alk. paper)
  1. Music—Vocational guidance. 2. Music trade. I. Title.

ML3790.G32 2005
780'.68'8—dc22
                              2004030454

CONTENTS

ACKNOWLEDGEMENTS

Thanks to my wife, Jennifer Pellet, without whose love, support, faith, and infinite patience this book would never have been started or completed.

Thanks to my parents, Naomi and Alfred, for creating a supportive family and building a loving household where artistic pursuits were encouraged, applauded, and valued.

Thanks to my brothers David and Jonathan for sharing their unique musical gifts, insights, and searing constructive criticisms.

Thanks to my Fuller bandmates, Mac Randall and Peter Catapano, for their inspiration, creativity, appetite, and unshakable friendship. And thanks to past bandmates Alison Johnson, Thom Kettrick, Rob Fitzpatrick, and Peter Clarke for joyfully enduring the bumps and bruises along the road less traveled.

Thanks to Andrea Rotondo for her generosity of spirit, encouragement, and trust.

To Sarah Pellet for her Kangaroo spirit.

To Matthew Benton Pellet, for reenergizing a bunch of jaded musicians and reminding them what musical passion is all about.

More thanks…

To Noel Tipton, Ted Schlossberg (my most influential music teachers), and the thousands of music teachers out there who tirelessly plant seeds in unappreciative students, keep them interested, and give them the tools to figure it out on their own.

To Wharton Tiers, Paul Johnson, Ben Forgash, and Harry Remer for lessons taught even if they never knew they were teaching.

To Laurie Jakobsen, Steve Karas, Aleba Gardner, Karen Wiessen, Peter "Chone" Primamore, Jay Rodriguez, Neil Gillis, Joe D'Ambrosio, Steve Ciabbatoni, Brian Turner, Bill Curran, Suzanne Glass, John Schaefer, Paolo Suarez, Frank Veronsky, Andrew Leary, Jim Walsh, Chuck Garvey, Derek Sivers, Brian Stoltz, Michael Robelo, Joan Hathaway, Marshall Jones, Martin Hall, G, David Wimble, Bill Benson, Judy Tint, Marc Schiffman, Romeo, Stinky, and anyone I should've mentioned but forgot to, for taking time out of their busy lives to speak, listen, offer favors, and share their wisdom.

Credits

Managing Editor: Andrea M. Rotondo
Copyeditor: Amy Blankstein
Cover Design: Josh Labouve
Production Director: Dan Earley
Interior Design: Len Vogler
Publicity Director: Alison M. Wofford

ABOUT THE AUTHOR

Michael Gelfand is a performing musician and a widely published freelance music journalist living in New York City. His music career started at the age of eight as a classically trained pianist, but thinking the clarinet was far cooler, he picked it up and became concertmaster upon entering junior high school. Tiring quickly of licking reeds and listening to stupid Benny Goodman jokes, he soon taught himself how to play the bass guitar and instantly fell in love. He has played the instrument ever since.

Gelfand has been an active musician in the New York City club scene for the past decade, writing songs and playing bass with his band Fuller in well-known NYC clubs like the Mercury Lounge, The Knitting Factory, and Tonic; as well as major venues in Boston, Philadelphia, Washington, D.C., and Chicago; and Austin, Texas' South By South West music conference.

Gelfand received a master's degree in journalism from New York University in 1992. Although he had written about music for high school and college newspapers, he didn't begin writing professionally about music until 1996, when he was asked to write a first-person "Expert Witness" piece about his experiences as a musician for *Musician* magazine—the experiment was a success, and he went on to become the magazine's senior editor and its primary New York editor.

Gelfand has written about an eclectic variety of musicians—and their techniques, philosophies, and strategies—from behind his desk, the cramped confines of transcontinental flights and tour buses, and from inside recording studios and green rooms nationwide for publications like *Esquire, Interview, Musician, Rollingstone.com, Launch.com, All Music Guide, Guitar World, Modern Drummer, EQ, Pro Sound News,* and many others.

Aside from music, Gelfand is a practicing karate student and an avid cook, as well as a notorious food snob and rum aficionado. He is married to Jennifer Pellet, founder of Inkstone Editorial, a custom publishing company, and he plays God to two solipsistic but otherwise lovable cats.

INTRODUCTION

In a perfect world, all any musician would ever need to do to promote their music is play a few notes and people would come running to listen. Oh, life could be sweet as a post-modern Pied Piper—packed houses every night, club owners begging you to perform whenever you like, unlimited encores, endless free drinks at the bar, and crowds of groupies and A&R reps fighting backstage to see who gets to suck on your toes first. Sadly, the world is far from a perfect place, and blowing a catchy riff on a penny whistle just isn't as sexy a deal as it used to be.

Being a musician these days is as much about actively promoting your own music and image as it is about performing and recording. It's an unfortunate but very real necessity borne out of the marriage between art and commerce. You may resent its existence, but you can't refute its significance. Like it or not, promoting your music and your image is at least as important as having chops and creativity like John Coltrane or Jimi Hendrix.

Believe me when I say I wish this weren't the case. Music for music's sake is a wonderful thing, but it rarely pays the rent. Despite what your heart might tell you, knowing how to promote yourself and your music will prove to be invaluable down the road. It might feel unnatural now, but you'll learn to appreciate the fruits it can yield.

For a taste of those fruits, look no further than archival video footage of young women swooning over Elvis Presley's swiveling hips and pouting lips. The riotous response he received when he performed perfectly illustrates the raw power of self-promotion. He could've remained tight lipped and stood stiffly onstage, but the King wasn't naïve about the effect his music and actions had on people. In his early days he drove women wild, and that, in turn, drove men wild. This had the effect of pushing Elvis to the forefront of cultural popularity while also pushing millions of dollars into his bank account. Things eventually got ugly when he started stuffing handfuls of drugs and all those deep-fried peanut butter-and-banana sandwiches into his mouth, but that's another story.

Conversely, go on line and check out video clips of Janet Jackson's right breast spilling out of her costume during the halftime show at SuperBowl XXXVIII, and you'll see how pathetically transparent the projection of an artist's image can appear when it backfires. Jackson's faux pas was blandly inappropriate, but not for the reasons over which would-be censors and the FCC got all bent out of whack. Relatively few people got upset upon seeing her exposed breast—they were upset because her "costume malfunction" did little to obscure the fact that her "dainty" performance with Justin Timberlake was a painfully irrelevant abomination. (Despite what many of our puritanical political leaders might think, some of us have actually seen breasts before and find them anything but offensive.)

When it comes to the act of selling records, knowing how to project a well-crafted image is critical to an artist's success. In Elvis' case, he had it all going on. In Janet Jackson's case, the jury is still out, but her little flashdance surely got people talking about her again. An artist's image can be sexy, silly, demonic, debauched, or anything that floats their boat, but if nothing else it needs to be effectively communicated. Sometimes an effort to communicate an artist's story misses the mark, but that's way better than not having anything worth talking about. For all intents and purposes, an artist without a story to tell has nothing to sell, and it's no different if you're simply trying to make a name and build a reputation for yourself.

You don't need to worry yourself about creating a media circus, just yet. For now you need to focus on the fundamentals of self-promotion: Writing, recording, and performing great music; networking; building a press kit; receiving local press coverage; and understanding how these projects will help you build a viable career as a musician.

It would be immature to think the world is going to beat a path to your door just because you can dance like Fred Astaire or play rapid-fire 64th notes on your guitar, yet so many musicians have felt this way at some point in their career. Sorry, but great talents aren't discovered by accident anymore. Once you've got the music in place, you've got to create a plan, lay the groundwork to execute it, and then slowly introduce a campaign that creates a buzz to let people know that they should care about you.

Harsh as it may sound, if you haven't already started doing these things, then nobody in the music business or general public is going to be terribly concerned with you or your work. You're probably a very nice and talented individual, but there's simply way too much else going on for people to go crazy over you without good reason. People have bills to pay, TV shows to watch, and books to read, and the folks in the music business are too busy worrying about the dissemination of illegal digital downloads, egregious copyright infringements, plunging CD sales, and layoffs to be bothered with little old you unless your independent release is making some serious noise on Soundscan's sales charts. (Nielsen SoundScan is an information system that tracks and compiles weekly sales data for music and music video products sold throughout the United States and Canada; it is the source for *Billboard's* music charts.) Nobody cares unless you give them a reason. Rather, nobody except maybe your mother, and she probably would have preferred that you had become a doctor or a lawyer.

You've got to build your career from the ground up. No one starts at the top. Start small, chart a course, find the current, get some wind in your sails, use its momentum, and start reaching out to people to let them know what you're doing. Once you've nurtured that career and developed a following, people might start caring when you shake your ass and flaunt your star-covered nipples on national TV, but for now you're better off making sure people know you're out there and that you're worth paying attention to. Getting all freaky on them is something you can try later.

I can't say it enough—image reigns supreme in the music business. It's what creates excitement around musical performances and helps generate sales of CDs. It also accounts for some hefty competition when it comes to getting people to pay attention to what you're doing. All of the media hype surrounding established artists, as well as those on the verge of reaching critical mass, creates static and dissonance that's difficult for relatively unknown artists to cut through. You'll need dedication, persistence, flair, and lots of talent to break down those barriers if you're going to have a chance to grab the brass ring.

Right now your talent may be your greatest asset, but all that talent won't matter unless you're prepared to play the game. That doesn't mean you can't play it unconventionally, but play it you must. Competition among musicians is fierce, with everyone trying to stake out territory they can claim as their own. We're all fighting for the same measly scraps of air-time in living rooms and record stores; at parties, local clubs, and concert halls; and on the radio, the Internet, and television. That makes it incumbent on you to find your lot and claim it before someone else snatches it away.

Writing and performing great music is a start, but the number of artists who can repeatedly get fans to cough up the price of a concert ticket or a CD on nothing but the power of their music is shrinking. You've *got* to do more than that. You've *got* to promote yourself.

Fact is, you might be a remarkably prodigious musician of biblical talent, but there are hundreds, if not thousands of equally gifted musicians and bands out there that will do whatever it takes for the chance to let Madonna stuff her tongue down their throats on the next *MTV Music Video Awards* show. With so many insidiously crafty, industrious folks occupying the deep end of the talent pool, you'll need a real advantage if you're ever going to stand out in the crowd and receive the attention you deserve from the music industry and the fans who pay to see live music and buy CDs. That advantage—the art of self-promotion—is what this book is all about.

As far as self-promotion goes, I'm not going to sit here and proclaim that I've got it all figured out. Nobody does, but I have learned a great deal about what works and what doesn't work through my own experiences as a performing musician in the trenches of New York City over the past two decades. Those experiences have directly informed the tips I'll be sharing with you about self-promotion, and if you're a musician whose aspirations still outpace reality, I think you'll be able to relate to where I've come from and where I'm trying to help you go.

You'll also learn quickly that I'm pretty opinionated, and since this is my book, I'm going to keep things that way. I'll restrain myself from the mawkish rah-rah crap you typically find in books of this nature unless it's absolutely necessary. I'm not about to pull any punches on you. I'm going to tell it the way *I* see it. Hopefully you'll appreciate my honesty. If you don't, *c'est la vie*. I can't speak for your tastes, but I, for one, like the truth served up cold. The music business is too tough and unforgiving for me to concoct some rosy, Disneyfied story that comes coiffed, manicured, and wrapped in a happy ending. I'd rather spell things out as they are in the real world, based on my experience and those of other musicians and industry experts. Meaningful insights and useful resources are the only things other than your own experience that can prepare you to promote your music and take on the music industry with complete confidence.

I've looked to balance out my perspective by speaking with a variety of artists and industry professionals who I've met throughout my career— performing musicians and music-business lifers who know the business and have seen what it takes to succeed in it. Their thoughts and experiences add even greater depth and relevance to the points I'll be focusing on in the meat of this book, and I'm indebted to them for sharing their wisdom.

I readily admit that I've never been entirely comfortable with the idea of promoting myself, and I don't completely trust anyone who feels okay about it. That doesn't mean I don't think confidence isn't important—it's enormously important. Like the old adage says, if you don't believe in yourself, no one else will. That's dead on, but I also believe there's a lot of room in music for humility, and it can be difficult to keep your ego at bay after you've been walking around telling everyone who'll listen how great you are.

Humility is the unspoken code among successful musicians. You can have confidence in your ability, but you should be grateful for the talent you've got and recognize that you can also always get better. You can always grow, and you can always learn something new from someone else. If you walk around thinking you're the greatest, it either means you're Muhammed Ali or that you're not open to new sounds and new experiences. There's only one Ali, and you're not him. So if this paragraph is resonating with your conscience, you might want to look deeply into yourself to see what's driving your egotism. Closed-minded musicians with superiority complexes usually have short-lived careers and don't make too many friends.

I'm not immune to any of this. I've had my share of struggles as a musician, too. I've practiced relentlessly (or not at all), week after week, year after year, for thousands of hours in dingy basement rehearsal spaces, trying not to touch or be touched by all the diseased cockroaches, malevolent rats, and rotting garbage. And let's not forget all the flakes, junkies, miscreants, and losers with whom I've had the misfortune of sharing these rehearsal spaces. Oy!

I've endured more frustrating gigs and unreturned phone calls from "important people" than I'd like to remember. I've made records that make me cringe just thinking about them. I've performed in front of thousands of rabid fans one night only to play in front of no one but an angry bartender a few weeks later. In a nutshell, I've played hundreds of gigs; tasted small, sweet successes; and been crushed by near misses and bitter, soul-destroying failures. But I'm still at it, because I believe in what I do, and I feel as though the best is yet to come. New York is merciless, but anything is possible here. It's shamelessly vibrant and loaded with fantastic musicians, unique opportunities, and chance meetings with interesting, influential people, and that keeps me optimistic.

Every city's scene is different, but in many ways every scene is the exactly same. There are musicians just like you and me everywhere who are working hard to break into the public's consciousness. It can be an obsessive, all-consuming preoccupation if you let it become that, but all you can really do is define what you're trying to achieve and go about pursuing it earnestly. The rest will fall into place if you're patient.

Just make sure that you've given some careful thought to what success means to you. There's nothing wrong with playing gigs for the hell of it, and there's nothing wrong with wanting to set the world on fire with your music, but if you're really trying to take your music someplace serious, you owe it to yourself to really think about what you're looking for at the end of the process. To paraphrase George Harrison, if you don't know where you're trying to go, any road will take you there.

chapter one

KNOW THYSELF

Your decision to build your life around your music will mark an important milestone in your life regardless of the level of success you achieve, and for that I'd say you should be proud. Most people struggle to hold onto their identity as they settle in to safe, but ultimately soul-crushing corporate careers, and they couldn't even imagine how difficult—and satisfying—it would be to follow their own artistic ambition. And if you ever thought, "Hey, if I had only been a _____ I would've made some real money," don't even think to waste your time on that again. Yes, you could've been a proctologist or something equally distasteful, but why bother?

That said, you can probably see now that decision was somewhat naïve. Of course no one starts out thinking they're *not* going to make it, and you can't be blamed for thinking you have the makings of Elvis. We're all positive that we're going to be the next big thing, that certain someone with that special something who'll make the world stand rapt with attention when we bust a move. But in most cases it doesn't work out that way.

When your artistic epiphany happened, you decided to chart a course as a musician—certain of your destination, unsure how you'd get there, but confident that you'd figure it out along the way. You probably felt it was your birthright to realize your dreams of success, but now, after having taken those first baby steps into the real world of the music industry (not the idealized nonsense that you see portrayed on MTV, after-school specials, and in movies), you've come to appreciate the true nature of the beast. Success, as I mentioned in the introduction, is relative, but if you attach any monetary value to it—as most of us do—you know that trying to achieve it is no cakewalk. Being a successful musician, or at least trying to become one, is far from a non-stop party. It's actually a lot of work.

Unfortunately, few of us realized how much work it would really take to make it as a musician when we were in the earliest stages of our journey. Back when I was starting out, being a musician was all about practicing and playing gigs—nothing more, nothing less. I lived to play music. I could do it all day long, every day, and I tried to do so as often as possible. I spent boundless reserves of creativity and energy playing and practicing, and hours flew by like minutes.

But after a few hard years of working during the day to pay my bills and rehearsing at night to pursue my dreams, I began to see that it was going to be a lot tougher than I had initially thought. Achieving the success that I wanted for myself (and my bandmates) was going to require rolling up my sleeves and getting really dirty doing things I'd never done and didn't know if I'd be any good at.

LEARN TO CRAWL

Back in high school, no one ever went so far as to actually spell all of this out for me. Playing music was simply what gave me a sense of self-worth; it seemed like the natural course for me. Unlike all those useless extracurricular clubs my guidance counselor urged me to participate in to boost my chances of getting into college, music was an invaluable outlet that demanded real creativity and initiated new, meaningful friendships during my otherwise frustrating transition into early adulthood.

Being a musician was considered off the beaten path for someone like me who grew up in a quintessential, white-picket-fence-with-rosebushes suburb, and while the far-fetched dream wasn't against the law, it may as well been. My parents, more than most, supported my musical ambitions, but my guess is that they always assumed it was an interest that would pass from obsession to lifelong hobby. Since no one took my goal seriously, there was no one to pull me aside and say, "Hey, you're going to have to bust your ass to make this musician dream of yours come true. Are you up to the task?"

The fact is, no one I knew at that time could have known whether I would be able to handle the challenges because none of them had lived the life I was about to go chasing after, so it probably wouldn't have mattered. And I wouldn't have listened to anyone anyway, so it's a moot point. I didn't know how much I didn't know about becoming a successful musician yet, and the mysteries only started revealing themselves a few years after I had begun trying in earnest.

SET YOUR SIGHTS

Clearly, you've already figured out that you've got to take some new, difficult steps on your own journey to achieve the success you've imagined for yourself. Unbridled optimism will help you immensely no matter what stage you are at in your career. Sometimes it's the only thing that will keep you going when times are tough, and trust me, they *will* be tough. You'll find it incrementally harder to muster that enthusiasm the farther along you manage to go.

You're going to need to stay true to your belief in yourself and your talent while you're building your music career. Playing music is hard. Promoting the music you play is much harder, and you're going to have to take some shots straight on the chin before you'll ever taste success. Confidence will help you through the rough spots, but you need to keep your eyes on the prize and keep clawing toward it while you figure out the best way to succeed. There will be a lot of trial and error, but through experience and by reading this book (and others, I hope) you will figure it out.

Some of the tools and methods I'm going to talk about will likely seem obvious to some of you, but even if you're already well schooled in the basics, these are things you'll always need to think about. They are the fundamentals of self-promotion—without them no one will take you seriously. To use the words of an old Paul Westerberg song, you will be "shiftless in idle."

DEFINING SUCCESS

You'll have to excuse me if this chapter comes off a little heavier on the metaphysical goo than you might have been expecting, but we need to get down into some soul searching before we dive into methods and strategies for self-promotion. I don't mean to push any self-help mush on you, but there's a philosophical aspect that you've got to come to grips with before you start using any of the tools and strategies that I'll discuss later in the book.

You need to start this process by asking yourself why you became a musician instead of a doctor, lawyer, or professionally minded, big-balling, shot-calling rainmaker that society (and maybe your parents) hoped for or expected. Or let me rephrase the dictum as a question: Why did you pursue a career as a musician when you had to know how difficult it would be to achieve success in such a cutthroat, competitive industry?

You chose to pursue music as a career because you love creating it, and the idea that you could be paid to do something you love is thrilling. Whether you're a weekend warrior or a full-time musician, the allure of success obviously motivates you. Otherwise you wouldn't have bought a tome about self-promotion tips and secrets of success for musicians. There's nothing wrong in my book, literally and figuratively, with pursuing success and wanting to enjoy its benefits. In fact, I don't think there's anyone who'd have anything negative to say about it.

The problem is, no one can seem to agree on just what success is. Take a peak in Merriam-Webster's dictionary, and you'll see what I mean. Webster's says it's "a favorable or desired outcome; the attainment of wealth, favor, or eminence," while also noting that its once primary but now obsolete definition was simply "outcome or result." What are we supposed to make of that? Success *used* to be an outcome that pleased someone, but now it *requires* some measurable monetary or cultural achievement? Why did the meaning change?

Don't curse Webster for this unfortunate modification. Blame the bean counters at record labels who reduce "success" in music-industry parlance to numbers and equations on a spreadsheet. They measure success by looking at how much money you've made from selling CDs, concert tickets, and publishing royalties. Industry executives may point to the number of units moved by some saccharine-sounding, Platinum-selling artist and trumpet that artist's overwhelming financial success, but the total number of records sold can't be plugged into a formula to determine the lasting emotional or cultural impact that music has for the artist who made it or on the people who hear it. They rarely give credence to intangible variables like talent, creativity, critical acclaim, artistic merit, and an artist's happiness. But I would argue that there are thousands of successful musicians who have not yet been burned into our collective consciousness by way of incessant spins on MTV or commercial radio or by having their bikini-clad cellulite emblazoned on the cover of *Star*.

DEFINE SUCCESS FOR YOURSELF

Success is a very relative and personal term. Maybe it means receiving a positive review of your CD in a local newspaper, or perhaps it's having an artist you really respect ask to record one of your songs on their upcoming album. Or maybe it's making enough money as a part-time musician to avoid holding down a monotonous office job that you would hate. Your definition of success might not mesh with the dreams that someone else embraces, but you don't have to trouble yourself with what other people want. You just have to be concerned with your own goals. And if you're anything like me, that's more than enough to worry about.

Unlike success, which is totally subjective, money is something that most people understand, and I can't think of a musician who wouldn't be very happy to receive money to play their music (especially when they'd be doing it for free anyway). But wealth alone doesn't constitute success. It has nothing to do with critical acclaim that you may or may not receive, or any personal and creative satisfaction that comes your way as a result of playing music. If money is what drives your art, then you might feel like a success by making a lot of it (or like a failure for not making enough of it), but otherwise money is just money. Surely it can be a byproduct of success, but money shouldn't be confused with success itself.

Sometimes musicians have the good fortune to make lots of money by writing and/or performing music that satisfies their soul. I'd consider them very fortunate, but such stories rarely occur as a result of pure luck. More often than not, those stories start with a musician or group of musicians flush with talent whose ineffable spark demands a broader plan to get their music heard. Such musicians think about what they want for themselves, plan a way to get from A to Z, seek help from those who can provide it, and do whatever else they have to do to realize their goals, moving slowly if need be, until they arrive at their destination (or somewhere near it).

Success is only attainable if you understand what success means to you, whatever that may be. I can't tell you what it is, and I'm not going to pretend to hold some deep, dark secret about how success can be yours if you're willing to pay any price. There are no special pills you can take and no handshakes with the devil at the crossroads that'll do the trick. There's nothing you can do that will guarantee a successful outcome. You've just got to know what kind of success you want for yourself, pay attention to what has worked for other people who have enjoyed similar achievements, and hopefully from there you'll be able to muster the energy needed to do all the legwork that's needed to make your dream happen.

My point is that success is relative, and the sooner you realize it the sooner you'll be able to bring your self-promotional strategy into focus. Without that focus, you're going nowhere slowly. How are you going to promote yourself if you don't know what you want?

I don't mean to be cryptic about success. It's just that success—or the pursuit of it—is inextricably tied to the hardships and struggles that most musicians will face as they try to build a genuine career. If you're thinking about making music your job or have already jumped in, you've got to know what all the struggling is for so that you can protect yourself from doubters, dissenters, player haters, and malcontents. You also need to remember where you came from so that you can adapt when necessary without losing sight of who you are. The idea is to take the right lumps and make something out of your struggles, rather than simply taking lumps for the sake of taking them.

What I'm trying to do here is give you some hard-won perspective on how to set about achieving success on your terms, whatever those terms may be. I can offer some different ways to approach success, but how you get there depends on the type of trip you want to take, how much baggage you're planning on bringing, and how long and hard you're willing to work along the way. Hopefully you'll get smacked hard by the luck stick, but to a certain extent you can dictate that, as well. As my dad used to say, "we make our own luck."

BACK-OFFICE BUSINESS

Playing music is the fun part of being a musician, but there's a practical business side to it as well, and being honest about this goal-oriented aspect of your career can be very difficult. Music is an art, but it's also a business, and if you're unaccustomed to the ways of business or politics, then you and your dream are going to get banged up, and that can hurt—a lot.

"Making it" as a musician has as much to do with business behind the scenes as it does with the music onstage or in the studio. Everyone likes doing the sexy stuff, but few people want to roll up their sleeves and get their hands dirty with the back-office drudgery, and that's a huge part of the equation that you'd better come to grips with. If you haven't already made yourself familiar with the non-musical aspects of your music career, it's time to get down to business.

It's natural to feel a little uncomfortable with the idea of turning your dream of success of a music career into a steely business plan with talking points, timelines, and milestone events, but that's a transition that any serious musician must make if they're going to get what they want. Most musicians have an aversion to mixing business with passion, but why is our passion any different from that of any other entrepreneur?

That's what we are. Musicians are melodic entrepreneurs, creating products that we think the world wants and needs to hear, and we've got to address our business needs seriously or else there's no knowing how to promote and sell your own product. If you're trying to be a success, why wouldn't you make every effort to understand your marketplace and use all the sales and advertising tools that are at your disposal?

I'm not blaming you if you didn't show much interest in business classes when you were in school. I surely didn't. I was into the arts—music, writing, and drinking during study hall hours, to be specific—and I never took finance or marketing courses because I never thought I'd ever pursue a job that would require such expertise. But I was wrong in more ways than one, and now I'm sorry that I didn't take those courses. I would have been better off if I had a little business background, but when I decided it was time to familiarize myself with the business angle of being a musician, I immersed myself in it and got a handle on it. You can do the same thing. That's a large part of what this book is about.

Acknowledging that you don't necessarily have business acumen is the first step to take toward gaining those skills. As a musician, you now have a context to apply that knowledge, but you're not going to absorb it all over night, so don't be too hard on yourself. You've got confidence in your ability as a musician, so have confidence in yourself as a thinker and a doer. It'll all come together, somehow, some way.

REALITY CHECK

Seeing your friends advance in professional careers as you labor ceaselessly toward the same elusive goal can make you question your decision to pursue music. And it's good to question your choices every now and then, but don't get caught up in comparing yourself to non-musicians. It's like comparing psychopaths to mannequins.

It's really hard for most non-musicians to understand or appreciate, but being a musician is not always as cool as it's cracked up to be on TV or in the movies. It's an alternate universe when compared to their workaday experience, but it can be one of the most difficult jobs there is.

Most people have jobs where they're required to arrive and depart at certain hours. They are expected to wear a style of clothing (yes, even on "casual Fridays"), and most of them work out of dehumanizing cubicles that reek of the smell of overheating copy machines, Krispy Kreme donuts, and stale industrial coffee wafting through the air vents all dreary day long.

Your place of work changes all the time, as do your hours and your attire. Sometimes you're practicing by yourself in the wee hours of the morning. Other times you're hunkered down with your bandmates practicing in some garage or putrescent basement rehearsal space during off-hours. Other times you're performing late-night gigs in small, no-name clubs or sweating through your clothes in some tucked-away recording studio.

In the 9-to-5 world, it's thought that a person who stays at the same menial job for too long and doesn't receive raises or promotions must either be doing something wrong or must not be very good at their job. That's simply not the case for musicians, but the rest of society doesn't seem to get it.

In everybody else's world, your lack of professional success (there's that word again) defies logic, and inevitably that perceived sense of failure creeps up in conversations. "How's it going with that music thing," they'll ask. Or, "What's up with your music," as if it were some disgusting digestive condition that might go away if treated with antibiotics.

After enough people confront you with the same question, it gets harder and harder to talk about the great song you worked out in practice that day, how horrible the soundman was at the last gig you played, or how you're starting to see more new faces at your band's weekly residency at the local hotspot. They can't relate to that, and instead you end up coughing up some self-deprecating excuse to placate them—if they don't think you're that serious about it, they won't worry about you.

Truth be told, it's often easier to pretend that you don't take your music that seriously because it dulls the pain you've endured along the way. Most musicians truly believe in their music regardless of what genre or style it is, but treating it less seriously somehow dilutes the disappointment and makes it easier to tolerate.

Start taking it seriously. You know you're talented and you want the world to know it. You've also got lots of company, and everyone else wants the same piece of pie, but you've got an advantage that they don't have. You're taking a hard look at yourself, tallying your strengths and weaknesses, and figuring out how to make the most of what you've got going for you.

So tell me again, why are you a musician? Is it because you love writing, recording, and performing music, and it's what you do best? Maybe you want the legendary lifestyle of sex, drugs, and overall excess. Or perhaps you've been doing it so long that you don't even remember why you're doing it, but you're smart enough to realize that it's too late to become a doctor, lawyer, or President of the United States (although our presidential candidates often make it appear that anyone could score that job), so you wake up each morning to fight the good fight for another day. Then again, maybe it's something else entirely.

Whatever your reason is doesn't really matter, as long as you have one. We've already determined that you're interested in learning a few things about self-promotion, but before you can move forward, you need to understand who you are at your very core and why you do what you do. That's the best way to decide which strategies will work best for you. No matter what type of musician you are, you can't play pretend. Know who you are before you formulate a plan, and you'll be well served on the rest of your journey.

I can't speak for you, but my reasons for being a musician have never been cut and dry. It's way more complex than that, way too multifaceted. For starters, I'm simply in love with the sounds that I can create with instruments, and I can't think of a better way to make a living than getting paid to create more of them. Whether I'm by myself or playing with my bandmates, music makes me feel complete, and I know that my life would feel empty without it. It's been that way as long as I can remember, and I don't expect to ever give it up.

TO BE, OR WHAT?

Is this a hobby or are you giving up the day job? You may take your music very seriously, but there's a big difference between moonlighting as a musician and looking at it as your career. Given the huge number of musicians out there and the small number of paying gigs that are available in the market, it'd be unfair to say that you've got to be full-time or no-time. Everybody's got to do something to make ends meet, and if those things include a non-musical job, then so be it. That doesn't make you any less of a musician. It just means that you're doing what you have to do while waiting for your big break.

Like the majority of us, unless you're living with your parents or sleeping on friends' couches, you've got rent or a mortgage to pay and a need to eat. And you've got to pay for business costs like musical equipment, practice space, and transportation to gigs. If you're not bringing in enough money through your music yet, you have to make some tradeoffs, and that usually means slogging through some job to meet the costs of your music demands. It might not always be that way, but there's no shame in it. In fact, it's often the most practical way to deal with your burgeoning career while it's in an early or formative stage.

And holding down a job doesn't mean you've got to hate it. There are lots of jobs that are music-related, and that's a good way to keep your head and heart in the game. Better to be involved in music than not at all. You never know who you're going to meet or what opportunities might arise through your job. If you're in the right place at the right time lots of doors can open that otherwise might stay shut.

If music is your hobby and you're hoping to turn that hobby into a job, good luck to you. It's not an impossible feat but it's a little naive to think that you can dabble in music on the side and make it big when there are so many musicians out there who are totally committed night and day to making it. Again, it's not undoable, but the odds are stacked steeply against it.

To reach critical mass with your art, you need to do so on a solid foundation of talent, creativity, practice, consistency, discipline, and follow-through. Most of us have the talent, creativity, and practice worked out, but the latter three virtues are harder to master.

The more you do something—practice, perform, write—the easier it is to do that same thing the next time out. Auditioning for session work, using diplomacy to book gigs with a difficult club manager, or even replacing broken strings midway through a set all get easier each time you do them. And confidence will take you a long way, but jumping directly into the deep end when you don't know how to swim can be very dangerous.

If you're expecting to immediately thrive, make sure you're ready for all the consequences of such a bold move. If you're not sure, ask the opinion of someone who's already doing it, and if you come to the conclusion that the time isn't right, spend your time now gradually laying the groundwork so that you can take that leap of faith when you've defined what you want and drawn up a plan to get you there.

Throughout this book I'm going to talk about a lot of different strategies you can use to further your career as a musician, but none of them will matter if you don't have music that's worth promoting in the first place. It's the music. Don't think it's anything else. You've got to have great songs; you've got to have great recordings of your music; you've got to kick ass when you perform live; you've got to have a press kit that packages your music in a way that the music industry at large can relate to; you've got to get people to listen to your music in clubs, on the radio, and on line; and then they've got to decide that they like your music enough to buy it. It always comes back to the music.

It sounds simple the way I've laid it out there, but getting it all together is no easy task. To be blunt, if your music sucks, you are dead and simply don't know it yet. So how do you find out? You record it as best you can and play it for people. You perform it and see if people bob their heads or run for their lives. The market will decide if it likes what it hears, and if you start attracting fans you'll know you're onto something. (If you don't, you need to figure out what the problem is and correct it.)

All it takes is some attention from the outside world to get the ball rolling. A good demo will get you some small gigs; a little buzz generated from some small gigs will impress bigger, better clubs with an ear to the ground; and once you start performing at premier venues, the media will accept you if they like you. Once they start telling the rest of the world how great you are, the record companies will be clamoring at your door and from there you'll have people eating out of your hands.

But you've got to start at the beginning. Write songs that sound like no one else. Practice as hard as you can, then practice some more. Go out to see lots of live music and figure out why the most popular bands in your area are doing so well, then come up with a way to do what they do but a little bit better. Meet the people who book the bands at the clubs you like and introduce yourself, then sell them on the idea of having your band play there. Introduce yourself to anyone and everyone you meet who has something to do with the business and tell them about your music.

Invite people in the media to come hear how great you are, then blow them away so that they feel compelled to talk about you as if they discovered the cure for cancer. Put together a press kit with all the goodies—a CD, a bio, a photo, and some press clippings—and send it to anyone who can help you get noticed. Pursue relationships with DJs and programming directors at college and community radio stations so that you can score some airplay. Send your music to A&R executives who have signed bands that sound something like you do. Perform at major industry conferences and showcase events. Use your growing credibility to play bigger venues in your town and renowned venues outside of your region so that you can expand your fan base, build your reputation, and sell more records.

Everything you do moving forward from here is about the music. Get it together, and when you know it's ready, make sure you flaunt it. You've got to be aggressive and creative about promoting yourself in this day and age. You've got to believe in yourself, and you've got to stay true to your cause. Achieving success in the music business is hard enough as it is, so you've got to start out knowing that it can happen for you if you play your cards right. It's going to be a long haul, but if your music is good you'll have a much easier time getting there.

chapter two

DEMO HELL

The music business is always in flux, constantly reinventing itself to maximize profits and stay ahead of trends. Today it's a more confusing and desperate business than ever before. CD sales are down dramatically, labels are consolidating, and the Internet has upended traditional distribution. It seems no one really knows what tomorrow is going to bring, but despite all the changes and wild transitions, one thing has remained a constant: Any aspiring musician looking for his or her big break must have a solid demo.

THE DEMO

A demo is a musician's calling card to the rest of the music business. It is a universally approved vehicle musicians use to shop their wares to clubs, managers, and labels. It's far more powerful than a simple hello or a friendly introduction at a cocktail party. It can be a powerful knock on the front gate letting people know that you've arrived. When that gate opens, you've got to storm the fortress and you'll need every advantage you can put your hands on to stay there once you're inside. There's no more advantageous tool to have in your arsenal than having a good record. Nothing you ever do as a musician will prove to be as valuable or fundamental to your cause as a great sounding, well-packaged demo or full-blown recording.

The concept behind a demo is simple, at least in theory: Record professional-sounding versions of your best material and creatively package them to demonstrate to the industry how talented you are and why you are worthy of attention. With an effective demo in hand, you'll have a cornerstone of your self-promotional tool kit taken care of, and from there the sky's the limit. Producing a great demo, of course, takes a lot of work.

The operative words here are "professional sounding," "best material," and "creatively packaged." When I say "professional sounding," I mean creating a recording with audio quality that is clear, appropriate, and acceptable for your target audience. Ideally, the demo should sound as good as those same songs sound in your head, but that's usually an unattainable goal unless you've got an unlimited budget and a lot of time on your hands. The realistic goal is to get it as close as possible to your aural archetype.

Your finished product might not end up sounding lush and symphonic, like some lost Brian Wilson record, but it should imply whatever overarching sound you're shooting for at the very least. Keep in mind that anyone you're trying to impress with your demo will be able to bridge the gaps that may exist between what is implied and what is realistically attainable. If they don't get it, they're not worth impressing to begin with.

The idea is that you'll be able to focus on making these few songs sound as good as is possible, and even so, you're trying to create a working model of your songs with the inherent understanding that it is polished, but not neccessarily complete. The true goal of a demo should be to provide the listener with a strong sense of your songwriting ability, your musicianship, your showmanship, and your vision. Not all of that can be conveyed through a demo, but a lot of it can, and you want to deliver as much of it as possible without overburdening the demo or the listener.

Anyone who's giving your demo the time of day has developed their own minimum standard to filter through what they're listening for— whether they're booking gigs in a new rock club or they're looking for a female rap artist who fits a certain style—they are listening for something in particular. If you happen to be that kind of artist, then you stand a fair chance of impressing them if your songs are good. But even your best material could fall flat if your demo doesn't sound right, and you'll be done before you've even begun in their eyes. Next! All the ass-kissing and BS in the world can't undo the damage caused by a bad first impression. Your demo has to sound great in order to be taken seriously.

Intelligible audio is a must. If it doesn't sound good, the listener will shut if off before your music ever gets a chance to win them over. No one will sit through crap; life is simply too short. If your demo has good sound quality, your audience will listen with a critical ear to gauge whether you should be given serious consideration. They're probably not expecting to hear an audio masterpiece. You can make disturbing, dissonant sounds if that's your style, but they've got to be recorded well. Your listener needs to be able to tell it's intentional.

If your demo sounds good enough, your listener will be able to figure out how good you might sound if you had limitless money and time. They'll hear how good the songs are and how great the performance is—that's the result you should be after. If the production values are acceptable and everything else is in place, then the demo will be suggestive enough to turn your listener into a believer, leading you to whatever the next step is in your relationship with them.

What are acceptable production values? Well, that's subjective to a point—some people like the intimacy of a simple but clean room sound, others like a raw, murky, and unpolished sound that gives off a particular vibe, while still others want everything drenched in effects, compressed, and edited until every last, nearly imperceptible flaw has been air-brushed out.

No matter what your preference is, I'd say the minimum basic requirement you should set for yourself is that when someone plays it back through stereo speakers, a Walkman, or an iPod, they get an honest reproduction of the sound and ambience the way you'd want to convey it if you had total control (which, by the way, you do). You shouldn't have to make excuses for why things don't sound the way they should. Instruments should be discernible from each other, and they should sound as you'd want them to sound if you were performing for Clive Davis or some other record mogul who could make your career with a snap of a finger. You're not recording on an Edison wax cylinder, after all.

A demo should also capture the energy and presence of a live performance and deliver it with the impact you'd expect from a CD that you'd buy on line or in a store. No one will expect it to sound as polished as Sting, Shania Twain, Missy Elliott, or Metallica, but your demo or record should have character that resonates sonically and emotionally, with overt grooves that can't be denied, confident introspection that draws listeners in, and a smack of originality. (A little bit of genius helps, too.)

Your demo should sound intense, focused, and purposeful, but it shouldn't sound so tight that it comes off as canned or uninspired. It should capture the emotion of your performance—whether you're a solo act or part of a group—and you should sound like you're on top of your game. And every effort should be made to ensure the clarity of each instrument on its own, creating an overall sound that lets the listener hear the entire band as one while still enabling them to discover interesting nuances in each player upon each playback. This should be your goal.

Recording a Demo

Figuring out how—aesthetically—to achieve the best production values is a big part of deciding how to record your demo. Choosing how to record a demo—where, and on what medium—is another problem, but it's a good problem to have. It used to be that there was really only one way to record a demo—you went into an expensive studio in the middle of the night and paid to have your music recorded, mixed, and mastered on reels of expensive analog tape stock. From that point you took your mastered session to a duplication house where it was transferred en masse onto cassettes or vinyl LPs that you sent out as a demo. In essence, you created a vanity record, and it was a very expensive proposition that only well-heeled acts—or musicians willing to plunge into debt—could afford to take a chance on.

Thanks to evolutionary breakthroughs in recording technology in tandem with dramatic reductions in manufacturing costs, musicians now have more than one option for recording. You can either record a demo in a studio or, if you prefer, you can record one on your own by purchasing the equipment and learning how to use it yourself. There are distinct pros and cons to each choice, and you'll find either one to be simultaneously frustrating and liberating. In the end, the only thing that matters is that you manage to come out the other side of the process you've chosen with a finished demo and a semblance of financial and emotional solvency.

WORK WITH A STUDIO
By going into a studio, you're essentially hiring people who have a dedicated space, professional equipment, and the apparent expertise to record, mix, and master a demo for you. This can be a fantastic experience and a great opportunity if you manage to find the right studio with the right gear at the right price. And yes, this does happen—keep in mind that the home-recording revolution forced many studios out of business, and those that remain have been forced to lower their rates in order to compete or simply stay in business. This is a sad state of affairs, but their bad fortune might turn out to be your lucky day if you're not ready to buy your own gear.

And let's not forget what a relief it is to walk into a studio and let someone else deal with the headaches. Sure, you're plunking down hard-earned cash for the freedom, but anyone who's ever set up amplifiers and a drum kit in a room, placed baffles and microphones, tweaked pre-amp and monitor levels on mixing consoles, wrestled with complex outboard gear, as well as all the other hassles and problems that inevitably arise in a recording session, will tell you that such work can kill your enthusiasm for actually playing. Sometimes simply not having to deal with such issues alone is worth the price of going into a studio.

I've had both good and bad experiences recording in professional studios. I've enjoyed it when the gear worked as expected, the room had great ambience, and the person(s) responsible for making the session happen executed their job(s) as if it were the only duty in life that mattered to them. On the other hand, I've been miserable in studios where gear was worse than advertised, the room sounded like an ice-skating rink, the amps had microphonic tubes or didn't work at all, when the person(s) running the show got too stoned and erased an entire take of a song, or when someone's lack of expertise and professionalism got in the way of my performance.

To ensure that you have a good experience in a studio and come out with a great-sounding demo, you've got to really assess your needs and shop around. Start by figuring out how much money you have to spend on the process. I'm not talking about just the act of recording, but the whole process—recording, mixing, mastering, and duplicating. (You don't have to do all of these things at the same place, and moving around to different studios for each step is a common practice and often a necessity. Of course while it can help you save money, doing so can definitely complicate matters.)

Once you know how much money you can afford to spend, start investigating studios that will be able to accommodate your needs without sucking up your entire budget in a day. (As cool as it may feel to record in Abbey Road, you don't need to record in a big name, topnotch studio unless you're making a statement record for a major label—forget about playing a star role and keep things cost efficient.)

With your budget in mind, make a list of local studios by looking at advertisements in local papers and on line, and by asking other bands where they recorded their demo. (Don't worry if everyone keeps telling you they recorded their demo on their own—we'll get to that option soon enough.) Once you've developed a sizable list, start by calling each one to get more details.

Ask the studios what services they provide; it's likely that they offer recording, mixing, and mastering, but you want to be sure. Next, ask about their rates: Hourly, daily, and lockout (blocks of full-day sessions that can't be interrupted by other sessions) for each live room. Then ask for an equipment list (amps, instruments, microphones, mixing consoles, outboard effects, monitors, recording formats, etc.) and the number and dimensions of each live room they have. Then ask if there's an extra cost for recording with one of their staff engineers or if that's included in the charges.

Once you've whittled down the contenders, ask the most promising studios for the names of some local bands that have recorded there recently so that you can contact them to ask for their impressions of the experience. If that approach doesn't work, reverse it by asking some local bands where they've recorded demos in the past—if they had a good or bad time, they'll be able to tell you why and that'll save you in your own research stage. Based on the information you uncover, you can probably narrow your list down to three studios or less.

Finally, you'll want to visit each studio to see for yourself what type of place each one is. Granted, it's difficult to tell what your demo will sound like based on how a certain studio looks, but atmosphere counts for a lot when you're recording—you're going to be cooped up in this place for many hours or days, and you want to be as comfortable and creative as possible.

Maybe you like candles, lava lamps, oriental rugs, and clouds of incense when you're recording, or maybe you like raw, industrial spaces. Each studio has its own vibe and reputation, and you can learn a lot by taking the time to visit the ones that sound most interesting on paper. You might find the description that's given in an ad or over the phone doesn't mesh with reality when you show up. Then again, maybe it does. You've got to find out for yourself, preferably before you've booked the session.

Once you've decided on a studio and booked the time, you should make sure to contact the engineer who you will be working with. Even if this is going to be your first demo, you should spend a little time with them before the session, or give them a room recording of your band so that they can at least familiarize themselves with your music and the sound you're going after; this can help them when you're actually recording, assuming their own agenda doesn't get in the way.

If you need to hire an engineer/producer independently, it'll definitely affect how much you can spend on the demo as a whole, but good engineers are worth their weight in gold if you can find them. And don't feel like you've got to slum it. Aside from the heavyweight contenders making Platinum-selling records for the biggest acts, virtually every engineer/producer out there will be willing to work with you if they like your music. I've spoken with countless "name" engineers over the years, and all of them like to keep busy making money and working with up-and-coming talent. If you can figure out how to contact them, do it. If they can work with your budget, it might be the smartest move you make.

Roll Tape

At this point, if you plan on recording, mixing, and mastering at the same studio, you're home free to start the process. If, on the other hand, you are planning to mix and/or master elsewhere, you'll need to search in the same way you shopped for a recording studio. Ask people for recommendations, check the rates, inspect the studios, and go with your gut. Keep in mind that many engineers don't really like having other people around when they're mixing or mastering. Despite your best intentions, more often than not you become more of a hindrance than an asset when an engineer is trying to tweak a certain sound just so. You'll have time to tell them what you think when they're done, and if it's not right, they'll work from your suggestions to make you happy.

As you go through the recording process, make sure to listen to the sounds that you're recording. You need to be certain they sound good from the get-go. The less work you have to do in the mixing process, the better. If you've planned a multi-day session, ask the engineer to give you a rough mix of the first session without any EQ so that you can listen back when your ears have rested outside of the studio.

Whether you play that rough mix back in your car or at home, you might hear things that aren't right or that can be fixed before they become a problem later on down the road. (This rough mix rule should be applied at every stage of the process, and you should make sure to give your ears and your head enough time to refresh themselves so that you're not burned out when you're trying to give your music a critical listen.)

With all of that in mind, the act of recording a demo in someone else's studio rather than buying your own gear and recording yourself reminds me of that old saying: "Give a man a fish; you have fed him for today. Teach a man to fish; and you have fed him for a lifetime." If you pay someone else to do it for you, you might come out with a great demo, but the next time you need to record a demo (and you will) you're right back where you started, pulling hundreds, maybe thousands of dollars out of your pocket to do something you could do yourself.

This really comes into play whenever there's a problem during a session. When you're paying for studio time, the problem seems to magnify itself because it takes its toll in time, spirit, and money. Essentially, you're paying for the time when you're recording, when you're late, sitting on the toilet, drinking a beer, or pulling hair out of your head because your guitarist forgot to intonate his guitar and all of his rhythm tracks are unusable as a result. If you don't have your act completely together and you aren't sure whether you're ready to go into a studio, the pay-to-play variable will hang over your head like a ton of bricks. Unless everything goes according to plan—and it won't—you'll constantly be watching the clock. In my opinion that's extremely counterproductive, because if things don't pan out perfectly you're going to be royally screwed.

RECORDING D.I.Y.
By comparison, buying your own recording gear and learning how to operate it is a much larger commitment in money and time up front, but unless you're only planning on recording one demo in your career, you might find that the big investment early on will more than pay for itself over time. Think of it as an investment in yourself, or, if you're more rigid, as a business expense. (You can write it off on your taxes as a legitimate expense—no joke.)

The world of home recording opened up to the average Joe back in the early Eighties when costly and cumbersome open-reel decks gave way to

4- and 8-track cassette recorders. The sound quality on the cassette recorders wasn't great (it wasn't bad, either), but the cassette multi-track units were a fraction of the cost of the reel-to-reel machines, they were portable and blank cassettes were cheaper. Subsequent digital multi-track formats like ADAT, MiniDisc, and digital audio workstations (DAWs) soon followed, along with computer-based hardware/software packages like Digidesign's Pro Tools.

With each successive technology breakthrough, the gear got more powerful and more affordable, and today these formats are ubiquitous in topnotch professional studios and in basement studios around the world. They enable musicians of every skill and financial level to record themselves. Even someone with a meager budget of less than $1,000 and the willingness to buy used equipment can gain entry into this marketplace. While this won't necessarily even the playing field between you and the professional studios, it gives the little guy much more control and self-reliance than ever before.

Virtually anyone with the time, money, and inclination has the potential to record a song that sounds nearly as good—production-wise—as anything on the radio with today's readily available gear. This is not to say that anyone can twiddle a few knobs and start producing hits—but the technology needed to make an impressive recording is widely available, even if you're on a relatively tight budget. With a small digital multi-track recorder and a few microphones that you can buy new or used in a store or online right now, you'll have everything you need to record your own demos.

It's not as simple as "add water, instant demo," but to my mind it's a far more cost-effective and satisfying way to go about things than going into a studio. It'll take a little studying and a lot of patience, and your first few attempts will probably frustrate you to no end, but as you become familiar with the technology and how to use it, you'll likely be very pleased with how well you can capture your band's sound and how professional your recordings can sound with you at the helm. Ultimately you'll find that owning your own recording equipment gives you the flexibility to record when the creativity and timing are right, and you won't have to pay someone else every time you're ready to do it.

If you don't already know how to record yourself, then buying gear with a hefty price tag and a steep learning curve attached to it can feel daunting, but I still think it beats going into a studio unless you need to get the demo done in a hurry. If what I'm suggesting makes sense to you but you don't know where to start, there are loads of magazines, books, and Websites that can point you in the right direction.

Magazines

Electronic Musician
www.emusician.com

EQ
www.eqmag.com

Mix
www.mixonline.com

Recording Magazine
www.recordingmag.com

Tape Op
www.tapeop.com

Books

Recording and Producing in the Home Studio by David Franz
Digital Home Recording: Tips, Techniques, and Tools for Home Studio
  Production by John Chapell
The Desktop Studio by Emile Menasché
Home Studio Clinic by Emile Menasché
Producing Hit Records by David John Farinella

Websites, Bulletin Boards, and Discussion Groups

http://homerecording.about.com
www.homerecording.com
www.recordingWebsite.com
www.harmony-central.com/Recording/discuss.html
www.soundclick.com/board

You will definitely need to spend time learning about all the gear, but if you've been networking properly with other musicians—a topic we'll talk about later in the book—you probably know someone who can give you advice on what gear to buy and show you how to use it properly (or who might even handle that part of the equation for you until you get your sea legs).

No matter where or how you choose to record your demo (in someone else's studio or with your own gear in someone's living room), bear in mind that you'll inevitably run into problems along the way. Maybe there'll be a mysterious hum that can't be pinpointed but must be eliminated before you can start recording. Or maybe the engineer will struggle to get the desired sound from the drums' overhead condenser mics. Maybe the vintage 2-inch reel-to-reel machine the engineer said would give you that groovy, warm sound keeps eating all of your expensive tape, or the fancy computer being used to record your session keeps crashing in the middle of takes.

Then again, maybe the problem won't be a technical glitch at all. Perhaps your band will waste an inordinate amount of time trying to nail a solid take of one of your new songs. A dog will bark, a parent will unexpectedly return home, the police will show up with a noise complaint, there'll be a city-wide blackout, the drummer spontaneously combusts, etc. Whatever the case may be, you should expect the unexpected and keep calm so that you can deal with each case accordingly.

Even the best-laid plans can be undone. You can start a session thinking you're going to leave with four songs recorded and mixed in two days, which is pretty quick if you're looking to do a professional job. But if things don't go according to plan—and they won't—and you realize that you've fallen behind schedule, you'll be forced to do one of three things, none of which are ideal. You'll either fail to accomplish the goals you set for yourself, you'll rush to catch up to the schedule you set for yourself (which likely means screwing up even more along the way), or you'll be forced to cough up more time and/or money to do things right no matter how long it takes. Talk about stress…

No matter what option you choose to take, you're eventually going to come out the other side with a demo. Hours spent recording, mixing, and mastering will hopefully result in an end product that fulfills your needs and lives up to your expectations (although it'll probably fall a little short in that department because musicians almost always feel that there's some aspect of their playing that they could improve if given the opportunity). All you've got to do now is package it properly and get it out there.

YOUR BEST MATERIAL

Let's get back to what I was saying before about the three key phrases you should keep in mind when making a demo: "Professional sounding," "best material," and "creatively packaged." As you already know, I can't say enough about the importance of good sound quality, but sound quality alone isn't enough to lead you to the promised land. That's because nobody is satisfied listening to great sounding crap except audio geeks and Mariah Carey fans.

Sound quality is just a part of the equation. Choosing the "best material" for your demo is another key component to the process. The problem is, "best material" is a very subjective term. You probably have a good idea what your most compelling material is, or at least which songs you perform with the most conviction, but you need to think about "best material" from the perspective of someone who has never heard you before and may choose to never listen to your work again if they don't like what they're about to hear. They will listen to a few of your songs if you're lucky, and if they don't think each one is better than the next, you're in trouble.

You shouldn't choose your best material based on how you'd like to be perceived—choose it by how you *are* perceived. You need to understand what people find most interesting about your music and use that to your advantage. Play to your strengths. You want your music to leave an indelible, undeniable imprint on the listener's brain—they should be singing your choruses in the shower, humming your riffs in the car, and mimicking your beats when they're standing alone in an elevator. The best way to achieve this end result is to choose memorable material that stands out for its excellence and uniqueness, but that's easier said than done.

You might have a favorite song among your material, like a particularly clever chord change or a slick change of meter from $\frac{4}{4}$ to $\frac{7}{4}$ and back again, but that's not something a typical listener will necessarily notice. They'll just like it or not, that's all they'll know. Don't try to win over one out of every hundred listeners with esoteric time signatures and experimental jazz dissonance unless you are pursuing some obscure type of success for yourself. Focus on your strengths, not your anomalies.

Your songs should have the potential to burn themselves into the brains of a critical mass of people. That's what defines a hit. If your demo has hit-making potential, you will have grabbed the listener's attention, and that translates into dollar signs in the brains of people who run the biz. That's what will interest a booking agent, a music journalist, or an A&R exec who pulls your CD out of a stack of hundreds, slaps it into their CD player, and is immediately hit over the head by your sound. Whether it hits them over the head or not determines whether it ends up in a pile of woe inside their garbage can or in a special stack reserved for demos that make that first cut. And that is a short stack, I can assure you.

Determining what material is appropriate and what material still needs work can be difficult, particularly if you've never recorded a demo before and you're hoping to use this first one to land gigs. Most bands or solo musicians quickly develop a sense of what songs are working by gauging an audience's response during a live performance. If the crowd erupts into applause after a song, and their enthusiasm and interest are palpable, you know you've got a winner on your hands; if you finish a song to the sound of silence, you probably didn't leave the impression you were hoping for. That doesn't mean the latter song is a bad one, but it's probably not ready to be showcased on a demo. Either way, take heed of the message your audience sends you.

Even if you haven't experienced enough live performances to read what the audience thinks, there are other ways to make the proper assessment—you don't have to perform live to receive this type of criticism. Get an opinion of what's working and what isn't by making a simple live-room recording of a rehearsal and give that rough, but finished product to someone whose musical taste you trust. When you do, give them a list of the songs in the order that they are played, and ask them for feedback on each song, maybe requesting them to tell you their favorites and the reason behind those decisions. Do this with a few different people, and you'll start to get a sense of which songs are hot and which ones are not.

If you do perform live often enough for people to build an opinion about your music but don't feel as though you're getting enough feedback to know for certain what material is working, make it a point after every performance to ask people for constructive criticism (although some people may take that as a license to give it following every show whether you want it or not).

I constantly ask people for their critiques of my band following a gig to learn how it sounded to them and what they didn't like about it—I'm not terribly interested in hearing how great we were even though I'd admit that it sometimes feels good to receive praise. What I really want to hear about are the perceived flaws; tell me what sucked or what didn't sound right. Just because *you* thought your performance was great doesn't mean the audience did, and vice versa. It takes an objective perspective to point out when a song isn't being performed as well as it could be. Keep in mind that the opinions you ask for might be completely off base or potentially upsetting, so you'll have to weigh the criticisms accordingly.

Whether no one's heard your music before or you're already a known entity, you should eliminate material that impresses you or others simply on the basis of its musicianship alone. Instead, focus on selecting material with obvious strengths that would be apparent and appealing to anyone who's ever walked into a club off the street or turned on the radio in search of some new, interesting music. Those people are looking for something engaging, maybe even something they can dance to, move their head to, or lose themselves in, and it's your job to deliver songs that fit that bill.

Sometimes certain songs simply turn out better than others for no specific reason—maybe a cup of coffee made the difference—and you have to gauge whether the quality of the song overrides a deficiency in sound quality. This is very difficult to do because you know what you wanted it to sound like, so that colors your impression, but good songs should preempt well-recorded songs that aren't as good. You can rerecord it later, but first you've got to get the gig, and you should do it with your best material.

Each song on your demo should highlight a specific aspect that will be memorable—each song should stand on its own with some type of spotlight on an instrument or some clever hook or chorus. Think of the stark riff in the Rolling Stones'"Satisfaction" or the intro to Michael Jackson's "Beat It." Maybe your band has a tremendous singer and you're capable of Byrds-like vocal harmonies, or maybe you've got incredibly witty lyrics and great melodies, or thunderous riffs and a drummer who is the reincarnation of Keith Moon.

Whatever the case may be, you should look to present catchy songs that capture the listener's attention from the get-go and allow your strongest defining characteristics to shine through. If those songs happen to feature astoundingly brilliant chord changes, a dazzling display of technique, or some bizarre math-rock progression that requires a slide rule to be comprehended, so be it, but don't sacrifice the obvious crowd pleasers for the sake of your own ego; you might be impressed with the end product, but no one else will be.

Remember, the demo you're going to make isn't only about what you think is good. (Yes, what you think is important, but what's more important is what the person who's listening to that demo will think of your music once the demo is over.) Your target audience will be listening to see if your music is marketable to *their* target audience. They need to gauge whether they can make money off of your music in some way, whether that means booking you for an opening slot on a big night at their club or asking you for more material to assess whether your talent is a freak coincidence or the real thing and deserving of greater consideration.

Keep in mind that this is the music business, after all, where corporate success is not built on the appreciation of art for art's sake; it's built on the bottom line of a quarterly financial report. That's what pays the bills and will influence how the people who ultimately have the catalyzing power and authority to accept or reject you in the traditional music business perceive your music. You don't have to play by their rules if you don't like, in which case you are an outsider with a harder, but not impossible road ahead. If you want the major-label rock-star dream, but are unwilling to recognize the criteria by which you will be judged, then you should get out now before things get any uglier. Break the rules once you're a club member, not when you're applying to join.

I'm not suggesting you have to undermine your own artistic integrity to get ahead, but you have to realize that people are going to try to make money off of you when they say they're trying to help you make money. Once you can consistently pack a club with fans or sell 500,000 records with every release, no one is going to question the accessibility of the music you write, record, or perform, and you will have total control over what you do. But if you're a relatively unknown act hoping to book a gig or create some record-label interest with your demo, you have to present music that satisfies the expectations of the people who are making money off of the audience you are seeking to reach.

Put yourself in that listener's shoes, and you'll see what I mean. Whether you're using your demo to get a gig or trying to garner interest from a record-label, the person who is going to listen isn't going to be a musicologist or theorist, and they're not going to care whether a guitarist shoots off rapid-fire 32nd notes in a Phrygian or Mixolydian mode. They're going to care whether people will pay money to hear your music, preferably over and over again. That's it. Your demo has to convince them to give you a shot at living up to their professional opinion or expectations.

Given all the considerations you'll have to make when selecting material for your demo, it's easy to second-guess yourself to death. The smartest thing you can do is take a step back and ask yourself what you're trying to accomplish with your demo. Then ask yourself if the songs you've chosen will help you achieve that goal. From there, just do what you think is best and keep your fingers crossed. You never know what's going to strike someone else's fancy, and you can only do what you do best.

No one knows your music as intimately as you, and you're probably excited about most or all of the new songs that you're considering for your demo. But demos are supposed to be brief—three or four songs at the most—so you've *got* to choose the best you've got. Using too much material waters down the desired effect that you're hoping to have on the listener. Just give them your three or four best songs and make them count—if they want more down the road, they'll ask you for more.

I've struggled with this decision many times over the course of my career. Despite whatever anyone ever says to the contrary, my favorite songs are usually the ones being worked into shape rather than the ones already under wraps. That's probably because new songs bask in the excitement and freshness of discovery before they've fully matured, and that quality diminishes every time you pick apart, analyze, and break down a song for public consumption. They grow tame.

Remember, no one is walking down Main Street whistling the new songs that are up for consideration on your next demo. And they're probably not even whistling your old songs for that matter, at least not yet. Outside of your band and your most dedicated, hardcore fans, few people really know any of your music. That, of course, is one reason for making a demo in the first place, but it's also an advantage. You have the opportunity to put your best face forward before anyone's had an opportunity to formulate an opinion of you. For this one moment in what will hopefully be a long career, you are in complete control over what people hear, and it's incumbent upon you to make the most of it.

That doesn't mean you should choose completely disparate songs to show off how diverse your talent is. You'll have time enough to show off your many sides *after* you've made a strong first impression with one focused style. It's great to be a fluent artist, but from a marketing perspective, such new talent is hard to sell. Genuine crossover talents with staying power like Ray Charles and Prince come around once in a generation, so concentrate on choosing three power-packed songs that will demonstrate your strengths and build your career from there.

You'll ultimately have to choose the material, either with input from others or based on your gut emotion, but if you decide to toss out all the criteria that I've already mentioned, heed this last bit of advice: Assuming that no one really knows any of your music, keep in mind that your older music has already been through the ringer of sorts. It has benefited from the polish of repeat performances in rehearsals and onstage, whereas new songs are usually raw and unrefined. The listener might not be able to discern if one song is older than another, but they'll know if one song doesn't sound as good as another.

You've probably rehearsed your older songs more times than you can remember and performed them live on at least a few occasions. They might not feel as exciting to you as they once did, but they've withstood the test of fire, and you know them inside out. As such, those are the songs you're most likely to nail while under pressure, and those are the ones you should choose from when you're determining your selections for your demo.

That's a very important variable to consider: Recording a demo is a pressure-packed experience. Sure, it's a fun process, too, but there's a lot at stake when the "recording" light goes on, and you want to minimize the stress as much as possible. There is something to be said about capturing the energy of a newly written song early on in its life, but trying to do so after numerous failed attempts under a multitude of pressures is at best a reckless crapshoot, and at worst a tremendous waste of time and money.

Think of a demo as a recording of a live performance, and imagine yourself running through a set list in front of hundreds of people while time—and money—tick away. If you want to make the best possible impression, you should choose the songs that you know you can perform flawlessly without any concerns, because when the time is up, that's it. If you or any of your band members are unsure about how a song is arranged or you feel remotely uncomfortable about the feeling it's conveying, it's probably not going to turn out very well.

Don't ever rely on "fixing it in the mix." Sometimes when songs aren't working it's just a temporary vibe that can be easily remedied with a little more practice or some subtle rearranging. Then there are other times when that feeling is impossible to ignore because the song simply isn't ready. Be honest with yourself, and don't waste time and money on a whim. Catching lightning in a jar is as difficult as it sounds

Getting everyone who is involved in your project to agree on the songs that should be demoed requires good taste, diplomacy, and a unified vision. If you're a solo musician or you're paying your band to back you, the task is somewhat easier because you can dictate everything, but bands that exist under the guise of a creative democracy can have a tough go of it. It's nice to think that such democracies really exist, but band members are notoriously opinionated and proprietary regarding what songs to put on a demo. (You may notice there's an odd correlation between the songs a specific member nominates for the demo and the number of those candidates they themselves wrote.)

Sometime competition breeds productive creativity, spurring band members to write awesome material in a good-hearted, sometimes unconscious attempt to outdo each other. Other times, the creative process becomes ego-driven, and in such cases your demo will suffer as a result of an intellectual property clash. Don't let that happen. Be professional and try to discuss the selection process logically so that you can iron out the problems and make the right choices. You want everyone to be invested in the project so that they give each performance their best effort. Without everyone onboard, you stand a good chance of running aground.

No matter what your situation is, you've got to develop criteria to help you make those choices, and everyone involved should agree beforehand to stick to them once the going gets rough. That's the only way you'll have any chance at creating a demo that serves the big picture. Remember, the demo serves the artist by presenting the best, most representative material to the uninitiated listener, leaving them wanting more. The songs you select should send a powerful message, not some jumbled mess of styles and inconsistent performances.

This may not sound that difficult, but I can't begin to tell you how many demos start out with the best intentions only to end up a nightmare. The strategy is simple: You should record three songs as well as you can. Don't make the mistake of trying to tackle more songs than can reasonably be handled in the time allotted. This is not an album—that comes much later, if you're lucky. Choose three or maybe four songs that are most representative of your sound, and nail them. If you've got time left over, spend it on overdubs or in the mix.

Finally, don't be precious about the demo. You should strive to do the best you can with each song, but you should also be realistic about what can get done in the time allotted. Don't belabor the process with extra mixing or overdubs unless it's absolutely necessary; it costs more money and the return on investment is rarely worth the physical, creative, or emotional currency you spend.

While you might not be as happy as you could be with the finished product—and no musician ever is—you will be the only person who knows why. Chances are the little glitch in your tone or the slight dropped beat leading into a bridge won't show up on anyone else's radar, and you've got to keep the whole thing in perspective. You want to get the demo out there. Set yourself some deadlines and stick to your dates, because you're still going to need to create the packaging and get the CD pressed before you're truly finished.

CREATIVE PACKAGING

You can't just send your demo out to the rest of the world as a raw, unlabeled CD. At least that's not what you *should* do, but surprisingly there are still some boneheads out there who think that simply finishing the actual recording is enough and that the music will do the talking. But chances are pretty damn good it won't be. The one exception is when you know the person you're giving the demo to, and it's understood that you're giving them your demo in its most raw state.

Packaging in general is big business, but widely available computer software applications and digital cameras have pretty much leveled the playing field between what you and the Madison Avenue big boys can design. With a few good photographs, the right choice of fonts, a well-conceived layout, and a clever design, you can create CD packaging that looks as good as anything you'd find on ninety percent of the CDs from major labels. You don't need a creative team of copywriters and designers working day and night to create demo packaging. You might not come up with something that rivals what the folks at companies like Colgate or Coca Cola can do for their toothpastes and sodas, but you don't need to. All you need to do is deliver the relevant info. As long as you do that correctly, everything else is gravy.

That said, it's incumbent upon you to meet the minimum basic requirements for packaging content if you want to be taken seriously at all. Anything above and beyond will be appreciated if it's well done, but you simply can't skip the key ingredients.

Anyone who's taking the time to listen to your demo will want to know the name of your act, the titles of your songs, and how to contact you if they like what they hear. Most importantly, they don't want to search for that data. It must all be clearly printed on the CD itself in an obvious location, as well as on the CD jacket insert and along the spine of the jewel box.

Many musicians fail to do all three of these things, and I can tell you with complete certainty that most of these demos get thrown away as a result. Either the listener throws the demo out without even bothering to play it based on prior experience with unlabeled CDs; they hear it, put it aside, and can't ever find it again because it's not labeled; or they find it but can't remember who made it and throw it away.

It sounds harsh, but when you consider that most unsolicited demos (e.g., submitted out of the blue without proper representation from a lawyer, manager, or producer) are systematically tossed in the garbage regardless of the packaging, you had better make sure that yours presents everything a listener is going to need if they want to get in touch with you.

Forgetting to put that information on there is akin to telling someone you're not serious. You wouldn't show up to a job interview in a clown outfit, so why would you want to look like a clown when you send your demo out? You're trying to impress people here, not turn them off, and if you can't remember to put your key information on your demo, then they'll wonder what else you'll screw up. Remember, nobody likes to have their time wasted.

Don't put form before function. An expensive, tri-fold four-color CD jacket with an embossed holograph of your band and an enhanced CD-ROM video says you probably spent a huge sum of money where you didn't need to do. Remember, it's about the music. Create packaging that helps your great-sounding demo stand out in a sea of similar products.

With all of this in mind, treat your demo as if it were the only one you were ever going to get the chance to make, then set about trying to achieve greatness. After making your first demo you'll inevitably feel that you can do better on your next attempt. Perfection is an appropriate goal, but it's also an elusive one. Strive to do your best knowing that the law of diminishing returns will always apply—the harder and longer you work, the more likely you are to be frustrated and disappointed by the imperfections that nobody else will ever notice. Set goals on a timeline for yourself, and do everything you can to achieve each and every one of them. Finally, know when good is good enough—nobody makes a perfect demo, at least not knowingly. When you've exhausted your body, your budget, your favors, and your creativity, it's time to call it a day. Chances are you'll have many more opportunities to one-up yourself in the near future. Go with the best you've got and forge ahead.

chapter three

BUILD YOUR FAN BASE

When you hear other musicians talking about building a fan base, they're talking about the process of leveraging their creative assets (their music and their brand) to generate more attention from the public at large. It's all about accumulating loyal fans, and the way you do that is by either becoming popular through a natural process of performing regularly in a certain area and building up name recognition over time or by creating the perception of popularity and using that until you achieve it. The former takes much longer to accomplish, which is why everyone wants to sneak in through the back door using the latter approach, but realistically, you've actually got to combine the two to make headway.

I've always recoiled from the idea of superficial popularity being so important to the success of my musical aspirations. The purist in me feels that popularity should be based on creative merit and nothing more, but as I've learned over the years, it just doesn't work that way. Creative merit may have a value to musicologists, critics, and diehard fans, but club owners, radio station programming directors, and nearly every record company that's ever existed don't give a rat's ass about it. Popularity sells, and that's what matters to their bottom line.

Ironically, the kind of popularity I'm talking about is what we all dealt with in some form back during high school. You know what I'm saying: One guy is deemed a loser because no one can see past his coke-bottle glasses, while some other guy ends up being the talk of the gym locker room because he's got the cool sneakers, the radical haircut, the big muscles, or the girlfriend in college. Yes, that's the kind of ridiculous, but overwhelmingly influential kind of popularity I mean. Is your music cool or not?

As you become an adult you realize how unimportant being perceived as cool and popular is within the context of living your life, but within the context of having a successful music career, it's even *more* important than it was in your teens. Whether your goal is to become a touring musician, a session cat, or a jingle writer, popularity is a key to success on so many different levels. It may not be success in and of itself, but it is the single-most important factor in how successful an artist can be.

Take, for instance, a hip-hop artist who "only" sells 500,000 copies of their second record after having previously sold five million copies of their debut. From a record company's perspective, that artist's sophomore effort would be deemed a failure in terms of sales figures, but that same artist would still be considered indisputably popular relative to the thousands of unknown artists who would auction off their own vital organs on eBay if it would help them sell a fraction of that somehow disappointing total. I mean, come on! A half-million copies of their band's latest record translates into roughly a half-million people who have at least a passing interest in what you're doing. Since when was that a bad thing?

Sales numbers don't directly correlate with longstanding popularity, but they are a somewhat reliable indicator of it. They also indicate a certain degree of success if you adhere to industry-accepted standards, but record sales don't always tell the whole story—bands like the Grateful Dead sold a respectable amount of records throughout their career, for instance, but their concert bootlegs were equally (if not more) popular, and they made the bulk of their living on the road. Many bands have sold more records, but few have had the longevity or generated their own cultural phenomenon with a large base of dedicated fans. Popularity and success aren't always defined by numbers alone.

That said, you want your music to be appreciated by as many people as possible, and you're obviously not satisfied performing to your own reflection—you wouldn't be reading this book if you were—so there's at least some need on your part to receive feedback from other people. The people offering the feedback are typically called fans (except for the occasional critic), and the number of them you have on your side is what popularity is all about.

There is no mathematical formula or definition that determines exactly what popularity is. People showing up at a club to see you perform means very little if it only happens once, but when those same people show up at that same club every time you play, that's a sign of popularity. It doesn't go far in saying how popular you are, but it's surely an indicator that something good is afoot. And it may feel nice when a friend offers to buy one of your band's CDs, but that's an isolated occurrence. When that same friend brings her posse to your next gig and they clamor to buy your CDs afterward and beg to be put on your mailing list, that's a sign of growing popularity.

There are lots of hard, cold facts that can be used as criteria to calculate a level of success already achieved, but it's never cut and dried. That's because there are also many intangible variables that come into play to complicate the matter of popularity. That's what screws our aforementioned hip-hop artist who "only" sold 500,000 copies, and that's what gets so many people worked up over nothing. But what do you expect when people try to mix art with commerce?

In the music business, your popularity and the size of your fan base are key. Club owners gauge your popularity by counting the number of people who come to see you perform at their club and figuring out how much they can charge at the door next time, versus the number of people that come to see other bands perform at their club and how much their fans are willing to pay at the door. Record companies and commercial radio station programmers focus on a band's popularity when trying to figure out how to suck disposable income out of consumers' debit cards through CD sales or to generate advertising revenue. But instead of getting all complicated, let's keep this simple and say that popularity is measured by sales of records, tickets, and merchandise, all of which end up in the possession of people who like your music.

So if popularity boils down to whether people are willing to peel money out of their wallets to hear and support your music, more people means more money in lots of people's pocket. So it should be obvious to any musician who's looking to enjoy a profitable career that having fans—preferably lots of them—is important.

I'm sure there is someone out there reading this right now muttering how having fans isn't important to them. If so, then you're either very naïve, very stupid, or just lying. I've never heard of or encountered a musician who went into the music business to remain anonymous. Sure, a few supremely talented artists ended up wishing they could be relative unknowns due to the pressure and attention their stardom eventually brought them, but everyone starts out seeking some small amount of success and notoriety. It's one thing to play music because it makes you happy, but if you want to make a career out of it you're going to have to become popular or you're going to struggle mightily.

Sadly, fans don't grow on trees, but in a figurative sense they can: If you prepare the ground, plant the seeds, nurture them with water and light, and do so with a measurable degree of patience, you can expect to harvest some fruit in a few years (or sooner if you're lucky).

Nobody plants an apple seed and picks apples the next day, and no musician builds a fan base overnight—it takes a lot of hard, disciplined, carefully planned work over a period of time. It's crazy to think it happens any other way, and when it does (oh, miracle of miracles) it's bizarre, not the norm.

Yes, there are some bands and solo artists who just seem to appear at the right moment in time. Just don't walk around expecting that to happen for you. (You can *hope* that it does, but don't go too far down that road without a backup plan or you're going to have a very unsatisfying career with a very disappointing ending.) It's much better to expect the worst, hope for the best, and do everything you can to get closer to the latter rather than the former.

You can't expect people to show up out of nowhere to buy your records and attend your performances simply because you appear on the scene proclaiming yourself to be the next big thing. You have to offer people compelling reasons to pay money for the opportunity and privilege of seeing you perform and owning your music, and these reasons often require time to take root. In order for that to happen, you have to produce consistently good songs and regular live performances, create name recognition (e.g., a buzz), communicate with existing fans before and after performances, reach out to potential new fans, and lots more.

KEEP YOUR CHIN UP

But before we start looking at your possible plan of attack, there's one thing that you need to keep tabs on—namely, your ego. As I mentioned before, few of us are satisfied performing to our own reflections. We're all seeking some form of feedback from the outside world, whether it's in the form of applause, positive reviews, record sales, on-air interviews, covers of magazines, Grammy Awards, etc. But on your own self-promotional journey there's a very good chance, almost unavoidably so, that you will encounter feedback that's less than encouraging or flattering. Whether it takes the form of simple disregard (no one showing up to see you perform, which happens to virtually every musician at some point) or downright negativity (boos or scathing reviews, for instance), you must ignore it and keep moving forward.

In your search for feedback, whether conscious or not, people will confront you with asinine comments. Sometimes they'll say innocuous things, but other times a critical comment, whether meant to be constructive or derisive, will cut deeply into your artistic core—but only if you let it. The trick is to suppress your ego so that nothing anyone says, whether good or bad, gets in the way of you executing your plan. If you know who you are and what you want to achieve, people can say whatever they want and it won't really matter. (At least not too much.) Letting your ego govern your thoughts and reactions will only cause you problems and prevent you from doing what you need to be doing. Yes, I know it sounds like some self-help hokum, but it's true.

Obviously this is a hard skill to develop because we're out there trying to perform at our highest level while revealing something significant about our artistic selves, and when somebody in the audience shouts out, "Hey, don't give up your day job," there's often an urge to lay them out right there on the spot—It's usually the same schmuck who stands in the audience shouting "Freebird" at every opportunity—but you shouldn't waste your energy on him.

The lesson here is that you can't please everybody, and for every goofball out there who has some smart-ass comment or clueless observation about your music, there are lots of people who will like what you do. Instead of worrying about trying to be something you're not in order to appease someone else's idea of what they want you to be, just be yourself and try every method possible to get your music to the potential fans that will like it. They're out there; you've just got to be persistent and stick to your plan to win them over.

Even if you're doing everything you can to be at your best, people might not immediately respond to your music. Or if they do, they might not respond the way you'd hope for. Some people might actually have a negative response. There are player-haters (people who are vicious toward you because they're jealous of your talent or success) everywhere. And there are always people who just don't have a clue. Club owners will treat you like crap if you don't draw a large enough crowd, bartenders will scorn you if there weren't enough people buying drinks and tipping them, and there's a whole host of other people with warped agendas who will be nasty to you for no good reason. Learn to ignore their comments, or develop an open mind and some very thick skin so that the criticism and cruelty rolls off. You need to focus on playing your best and finding your audience, and unless you develop a tough exterior you'll be hard pressed to move forward whenever you encounter criticism.

RALLY THE MASSES

The paradox of becoming popular and attracting fans is that it's hard to reach critical mass, let alone get people to pay attention, when you don't have any fans. You must have fans to attract fans. For whatever reason, having a receptive audience in the room when you play validates you for other people who might otherwise be afraid to listen to their instincts.

In a fair world, fans would be a byproduct of raw talent and ability showcased on a stage with a few microphones, some instruments, and forty-five minutes of undivided attention from an open-minded audience, but the world is not fair and the entertainment business just doesn't work that way. Popularity is as much about perception as it is about talent. There is no universally accepted standard for it—talent is a subjective observation influenced by the masses whether you're judging yourself, another musician, or being judged by someone else.

If you think there are some musicians who acquire fans simply by showing up, you are mistaken. Sure, there are some people who have so much talent, charm, creativity, and beauty that they seem to generate a fan base effortlessly, but knowing—or learning—how to take advantage of those assets is usually what makes the difference for such fortunate artists blessed with obvious advantages. The rest of us usually have one or more of these attributes, and we simply have to work harder to develop some or all of the others. Regardless of what assets you bring to the table, the key to building a fan base starts with how well you create the perception that you're already popular or deserving of popularity.

CALL OUT THE TROOPS

The easiest, most practical, and obvious way to start building a fan base is to call on your legions of friends and family for their support. Whether you're ashamed to grovel or totally shameless, there's no better way to get yourself a packed house than by calling on your friends and family. Just ask them to come out.

They'll come because they know you, they like you (hopefully), and they have an idea of how hard you've been working and how serious you are about your career. If anyone is going to support you early on, it's them. Don't be bashful—ask them for their early support and you'll get it, and if you don't, demand it. Believe me, packing a club with rabid supporters will help you nail down your next gig, and if you use the momentum properly it'll lead to bigger and better gigs down the road.

Of course, it's easy to spot when a band has called out the troops in support. Inordinate enthusiasm regardless of how good or bad a song was is one clue, and there's often too many casual, back-and-forth conversations between the band and the crowd. (Interacting with an audience is good if it's brief, but it's not a good idea to get caught up in juvenile bantering and off-color minutiae when you're supposed to be performing.)

Use that early support to help build a larger fan base that's truly invested in you and your music. Your friends and family are best qualified to serve as a catalyst to attract these new fans—their unconditional appreciation will serve as a springboard early on, and they'll surely be there when you've hit the big-time, but only if you can take advantage of their presence when you're trying to grow.

No one would deny that playing to a rigged audience can feel good, but it's just a springboard. You should be trying to appeal to people who may have simply come out to see live music, walked into the club, and saw you onstage performing to a packed house. That'd make any music fan stop and take notice, but once band members start engaging in familiar conversations with buddies out in the audience, people will be much less inclined to think you're worth sticking around for. That's like turning on the house lights in the middle of the song—it's a buzz kill.

Don't rely on your early adopters for too long without trying to bring in people from the outside. When you're starting out or looking to grow beyond your current status, any warm body will do, but you've got to preach your gospel to the uninitiated rather than just to the choir. And you want to begin doing it as quickly as possible.

The goal is to develop a fan base consisting of people from all around your region, or better yet, all around the country, who don't know you personally and will come to see you perform whenever you're in town simply on the basis of liking your music. When you rely solely on friends who show up to support you, the turnout for each show will eventually wane, then become inconsistent, and then bottom out. That's no way to build a reputation.

DON'T BELIEVE THE HYPE

Sadly, many bands mistakenly start believing the hype from friends early on and rely heavily on the ready adoration of family and friends. They'll slather you with praise at first, but will likely prove to be an unsustainable resource as you progress with you career. Don't dig yourself into this hole. Start developing as many fans as you can from your first gig on so that when the loyal brigade scatters, you've still got support from other sources.

Once you've exhausted your closest friends' patience and good graces—and believe me, they will tire of supporting you for every show and eventually stop coming out regularly—the rampant enthusiasm you've grown accustomed to will not be there without real fans. So instead of stooping to guilt trips and asking for favors when the tide starts to turn, be proactive early on and begin attracting fans from outside your immediate circle.

How should you do that? Well, if you've done a good job of impressing your friends and family with your performances, the next step should be very easy to make. Start by asking each friend to bring someone along the next time they come to see you play, and make sure you mention that you'll put them on the guest list if they do. That new person will be pre-inclined to like you because their friend wouldn't have invited them if you sucked.

If your friends say they can't invite anyone, ask them to do it next time you perform, but if they come through for you and bring people, you should pay their admission at the door or put them on your guest list. It's the right thing to do because it gives them an added incentive to show up, especially if they were likely to do so anyway. If a club doesn't let you have a guest list, pay for their ticket out of your own pocket—while it might cost you a few extra bucks, it's a cost-effective way to spend your money. (It's like the bartender who buys you a drink after you've already had a couple—you'll be more inclined to buy another one when you're done and you'll probably come back again some other time, too.) And when you see them walk in with their friends, make sure you thank them for coming. Be a gracious, grateful host. You want them to know you appreciate their loyalty and effort, and doing so will make it easier to ask them to do it for you the next time.

WORK THE MAILING LIST

Another effective method for building your fan base is to create a sign-up sheet for interested fans to get onto your mailing list: This includes people who've been supporting you from the beginning, as well as anyone else who's interested. This may seem like a very simple idea, but you'll come to understand that it requires a lot of attention and responsibility from someone in your band or a closely associated delegate. Someone will actually have to manage that list and create something worth sending out to the people who sign up. It's tedious and very unglamorous work, but it's absolutely worth doing.

Creating the template for a mailing list is easy. Keep it as simple as a piece of paper on a clipboard with hand-drawn rows and columns for names, e-mail addresses, and phone numbers. Getting people to sign up is the hard part. Someone has to be responsible for carrying the sign-up sheet around toward the end of the show or just before your last song. Letting people in the audience know it exists is the key.

The trick is finding a way to offer the list to those who want it without making everyone else feel like you're forcing it on them—if people liked the show and want to be informed the next time you're playing, they'll sign up. You shouldn't have to twist anyone's arm. Just make sure you let people know what it is. (If you shove the list in people's faces and they're not interested, they're likely to submit false information that'll only waste your time when you're managing the list down the road.)

Whoever you designate to handle the actual list should carry it around from table to table, along the bar, and through the crowd to make sure that anyone who's potentially interested knows it exists and where it is. And they should be matter-of-fact about it: "Here's the band's mailing list. Do you want to sign up to receive information about upcoming gigs?" From there, let the people decide. Some people may need reassurance that you're not going to spam them via e-mail or call them incessantly, others may just need a little nudge to get them to sign up. Either way, you'll be surprised how many people will sign up if given the opportunity.

Once the show is over, you'll need to take the sheet home and enter the new information into some sort of computerized database or, at the very least, into a legible document, so that you can automatically send out flyers or e-mails to everyone on the list before each subsequent gig.

Whether you've got a significant mailing list or not, you should be promoting any upcoming shows. It's not necessary to do it too far in advance, and in fact it's a bad idea to do so because most people will likely forget about it by the time it occurs if you're too premature. Typically, seven to ten days of advance notice is plenty of time to let people know you're performing, and you should plan on making follow-up phone calls and/or e-mails a day or two before the gig. The point is to let people who are interested know the date, time, and location of the venue.

COLD CALLS

If you're like me, you'll quickly realize that this practice of talking yourself up to other people to get them to your show is a necessary evil, especially if you live in an area where there are a lot of entertainment options. No one really enjoys calling up someone out of the blue and asking them to come see their band perform—in effect, you're saying, "Hey, would you block out a couple hours of your evening to come pay money and support my band?"

The trick is to keep it as professional and matter-of-fact as possible. Call the person up, exchange some pleasantries, and just let them know the details. And make sure they know there aren't any strings attached. A simple, "Hey, we're playing tomorrow night and we'd really like to see you there," will suffice. Make sure they're aware how much you'd appreciate their support. Don't pressure them to answer right then and there. Just make certain they know the details, then move on.

The critical thing is to be yourself when you're lobbying for support unless you are painfully shy and have no choice but to force it. If you come off as insincere, people will pick up on it and will probably be less inclined to come out. If they know you're just letting them know and asking from the heart, they'll take you seriously and consider your request.

Keep in mind that there's nothing wrong with asking people to come or reminding them about a gig that's coming up in a few days. If they've told you that they like what you do or intimated any interest at all, you should absolutely let them know. It's a lot easier to keep an existing fan than it is to find a new one. It may turn out that only five people out of every hundred you call actually show up to a specific gig, but if those people each bring two other people with them, and those other people like your show, all the phone calls were well worth the effort. And if you keep up this practice, you'll give existing fans a breather and attract news ones each time you perform. Do like the farmers do: Rotate the fields, rotate the crops, and keep things growing efficiently without robbing the soil.

FLYERS AS A PROMOTIONAL TOOL

You should also consider creating some sort of postcard-size flyer containing all of the relevant information about the upcoming gig that you can carry around and hand out whenever the opportunity arises. It's as simple as dividing a an 8½" x 11" piece of paper into quarters, clearly writing info about your gig on each one along with a logo, perhaps, and bringing that sheet to the nearest Kinko's for reproduction on card stock; they'll even cut them for you. The reason I say you should consider this, rather than advise that you should definitely do it, is because there are too many variables that can affect whether this will be a worthwhile expense and activity for you.

Back before the Internet, reminding people about gigs was much more difficult. Many bands would print up thousands of flyers in order to blanket an area with the details. They'd place them on tables and in bathroom stalls inside clubs, put stacks of them on bars and entranceways, and they'd hand the rest out on the street or send them to fans in the mail. That was then, this is now.

With the advent of e-mail, you should view flyers only as an additional tool to get the word out, not as a primary one. It takes lots of time to disseminate them and isn't particularly cost-effective, but if you think it's worth the extra effort, try it out over the course of a few gigs and measure the results by gauging the turnout. (The best way to do this is to offer discount admission—a dollar or two at most—for anyone who shows up with the flyer in hand. You'll need to work this out with the club beforehand. They will probably subtract the discounted difference from your door percentage at the end of the night, but it'll give you a good idea of whether the flyers are worth the effort and cost.)

I do think giving someone a physical reminder about your show is a good idea, but it's probably more important to pick up the phone or send an e-mail these days. Just remember to keep the message simple, with the name of your band, the date and time you'll be playing, the name, address, and phone number of the venue.

FIND QUALIFIED FANS

It's definitely not necessary to stand out on the street corner randomly handing out flyers to anyone who'll take one. Most people will grab anything if it's handed to them, but ninety-nine percent of what you hand out will end up on the sidewalk or in the garbage can. The likelihood that some random person will actually take the flyer from you, read it, and decide to show up is very low, and you'll only end up wasting time and money.

It's much smarter to stand outside the club you'll be performing at a few nights beforehand, preferably on a night when a similar band is playing, to hand out the flyers. Or go to a record store or a bar where people who might like your music would hang out. You're trying to target people who are pre-inclined to like your music; they're qualified fans, and they should be an easier sell than some random person on the street corner.

If the club you're playing at is notorious for starting its sets late, let people know verbally when you hand them the flyer. If, on the other hand, the club runs a tight ship and manages set times very strictly, you should make sure to note that your set will start promptly. It may seem like an insignificant issue, but you don't want people to show up when your set is over, and they surely don't want to sit around for fifty minutes before your set begins. You're showing them a little courtesy, and in return you'll gain their trust for future gigs.

SAMPLES AND OTHER FREE STUFF

Instead of handing out flyers, some bands actually give away music or band-related items in an attempt to attract new fans. While it is admittedly risky in the short term (you could be throwing money away if people don't like it), there's a tremendous upside if you are willing to spend your money. You'll receive an exponentially more valuable asset than the cost of a single CD or cassette if they like your music and start coming to your shows.

Just about anybody with a computer can create his or her own CD or cassette sampler at home these days. There are kits that can be readily purchased in stores and on line to help you create artwork and provide you with the necessary materials, or you can bring a production-quality demo and artwork to any duplication or reproduction facility to have them do it for you. (This latter option is usually more expedient, but you pay a lot of money for the expertise.)

Economics will probably dictate how you make the sampler, but don't think of it as putting together a CD that you intend to sell. First of all, it's a freebie, so don't give away all your material. Like a demo, it should include three of your best songs, some simple but interesting artwork, and all the relevant band info (especially a contact phone number, e-mail address, and band URL). That's all anyone will need to decide whether they like your music, want to see you perform, or want more information.

Getting people to the gig is tough, but you should never forget that your actions onstage will do more to build your fan base than any other activity. You want people to return time and time again—in the retail world it's called repeat customers. You want repeat customers, and you want them to recommend you to their friends.

BUILD YOUR OWN STREET TEAM

The operative word I mentioned above is "team." In order to succeed you need a team of enthusiastic fans who believe in you and will help you do whatever it takes to achieve greater success than what you've got right now. It's easier to accomplish your goals when you have other people helping you along the way, and that's especially true when you're building your own fan base.

For years now savvy musicians have enlisted the help of devoted followers to help them get the word out about their music—namely street teams made up of young fans who love the music so much that they'll give up their own time to publicize your band. Hip-hop artists were the first to recognize and harness the street-level, grassroots power of these teams, and the rest of the music industry soon followed suit. These days, major record labels hire street-team companies to help create a message that can be spread virally—through word of mouth, flyers, posters, calling in requests to radio stations, and handing out free merchandise—to publicize record releases of large acts and shows of smaller acts.

These companies charge a lot of money for the services they offer, putting them well out of reach for all but the most affluent unsigned bands, but that doesn't mean you can't create a street team of your own. In theory, at least, all it takes is understanding how to create and then manage your network of street teamers, and since you're gathering contact info of every fan who comes to your shows and making a point of talking to them at those shows, you should have a pretty good idea who your most avid supporters are.

The way you create the team is simple: Pull aside your most fervent fans and tell them what you're planning. Explain why you need their help. If they're already rabid about your music, they'll salivate over the prospect of being welcomed into your inner sanctum. Think about it—what kid or young adult doesn't want to be a part of something that's going to be bigger than big? If they feel that they discovered you before you become popular and sense that their efforts could play a part in helping to break your act in the public's consciousness, they will invest their energy, enthusiasm, creativity, and muscle in support of your every move. That type of commitment is well worth any incentive you could ever offer them.

You don't need hundreds of people to start a street team. A handful of preferably young, energetic people will do nicely. Offer them whatever you think will motivate them to help your cause, and tell them the same offer holds true for any of their friends who they can convince to become part of your team. What can you offer them? How about free entrance to every show you play, or a signed, advance copy of your CD before you start selling it publicly? Maybe an invitation to your rehearsal space for a private listening party. These things might seem trivial to you, but to an enthusiastic fan these rewards are invaluable and will only strengthen their loyalty toward you.

Once you've established leaders for each group within your network, interact with them on a regular basis (maybe twice a month until things really get cooking) via phone and e-mail or at gigs or before/after practice. Let them know about upcoming shows and any notable news, provide them with materials (cassettes, CDs or mp3s, posters and flyers, tchotchkes, etc.) to do their job, and give them the attention, respect, and support to make them vested partners in your success.

"The kids should help you create the messaging," says Andrew Leary, COO of StreetWise Concepts, a Los Angeles-based firm that's developed successful grassroots support for bands like Deftones, P.O.D., Papa Roach, and Foo Fighters, among many others. "The whole idea is to get them excited and keep the message top of mind. There's a lot of music out there that people can get a hold of. Loyalty among artists is nowhere near where it used to be, so if you find people who are excited and you can engage them meaningfully with your music and images, then you give that person a reason to talk to others about it. That gives them some ownership," he says, "and they'll be more likely to tell other people about you."

Unlike commercial street-team companies that compensate their network of "fans" to support and work for a client, you are trying to create a street team that supports you because they want to. Your street team members won't expect money to pass out samplers in front of a show— they'll do it because they believe in what you're doing and are therefore getting something more substantial back from you. The prospective fans who take the samplers from them will do so because they'll know that the enthusiasm they're seeing is credible.

Newer, relatively unestablished bands actually stand to benefit a great deal from a street team, says Leary. "When kids can discover something they don't know about, there's a real possibility to get a viral movement started. Young bands have got to keep a dialogue with every person who's ever expressed interest in them. That's basic marketing. That's customer acquisition. Once you acquire them, you have to keep them. A strong base will help you build a strong viral campaign."

But remember, credibility is the key component to your street teams' success. They will be less likely to interest anyone else in your music unless they're interested themselves. "It's like the person in the department store spraying perfume on all the women walking by," explains Leary. "If you're not interested, you're not interested, and it doesn't matter if it's for free." Credible people talking about your music to other people gives you credibility, and that's what you need to build a relationship, develop a dialogue, and get more and more people to become invested. Turn a few people into true believers and they'll want to tell everyone about you.

Attracting fans and building a fan base is very difficult whether you perform in a bustling metropolis or in some extremely remote, rural area. Granted, these two extremes are radically different from each other, but the one thing they share in common is a reliance on people. In large cities, there are lots of people living in a condensed area, but they have lots of choices on how they can spend their time. In rural areas, there aren't a lot of entertainment options, but each one is miles apart from the others. Regardless, in both cases you still have to convince people that you provide the best option for their entertainment dollar.

So how do you get them to care? First you've got to get "them," and that's the hard part. The best way to get people interested is to be good. Be *very* good. Even if you're playing your first show, you've got to create an aura of excitement that gets—and keeps—your loyal following (friends, family, significant others, colleagues from work) interested, because they are the ones that will provide you with an attentive critical mass early on. They will applaud your every move, and that will get the attention of people who didn't necessarily come out to see you but happen to be in the venue.

chapter four

THE NETWORK

It's often said that cream rises to the top, but if you watch MTV at any given hour of the day or night it's apparent that crap rises to the top, too, and with much greater frequency. How can that be possible? Well, it's simple: It's not what you know about music that counts, but *who* you in the music business know that matters most.

That's not to say that a load of talent or deep knowledge of music theory doesn't bring anything of value to the music you play and perform, but groundbreaking creativity, blistering technique, and a complete understanding of scalar modes and intervals won't give you any meaningful advantage in the business side of the music world. There are thousands of tremendously talented players out there all grabbing for the same prize, so you're going to need all the help you can get. That's why nothing is more instrumental to your success than working hard at networking.

How is that possible? One well-placed acquaintance can do more to jumpstart a successful career than a lifetime of practice. I'm sure music teachers everywhere will collectively puke after reading that line, but musicians rarely land big record deals simply because they practice the hardest. More often than not, the person who makes it big is someone who practices hard and networks even harder—or hires someone to network for them.

It's naive to think that success is about the music and nothing else. Talent is a critical factor, but without help from people along the way—friends, colleagues, associates, and power brokers in high places—your road will be much, much harder. Knowing how to get the attention of someone who can offer you a floor to sleep on while you're out on tour is all about networking. So is knowing and meeting the players and power brokers in the industry— the music critics, the radio program directors and disc jockeys, the A&R folks, the owners of indie record labels, booking agents, tour promoters, etc. And just knowing these people isn't enough. Networking is meeting them and keeping those relationships fresh and vital over the years. That's what eventually makes the difference between anonymity and a lucky break. The network you build over time can provide the catalysts you need to get a tremendous leg-up on everyone else. Unfortunately there's no single way to do it, and you will have to feel it out as you go, but there are some basic tenets to keep in mind as you make your way.

But before we go there, remember that simply knowing one person who's got juice in the biz doesn't necessarily do you any good. If you bet all your hopes and dreams on one person and they lose their job before you can ask for a favor, or if they try to deliver and fail, you're screwed. You need to know as many people in the business as you can, both big fish and small fries. You want them all to know you, respect you, like you and—most importantly—want to help you succeed. They should be local, regional, and national contacts, and if at all possible, you want them to feel the same way about needing you as you do about needing them.

POP THE QUESTION

Networking is the key that will unlock your potential, but only if you make use of the cumulative power that exists in your network once you've built it. In simpler terms, you've got to ask people for help. Don't be bashful. Be specific and offer an action plan listing three ways they can help your career. Knowing the right people does you no good if you don't ask them to help.

Ask and ye shall receive—just as long as you don't ask too often. Sometimes it's best to wait until you're absolutely sure you need the help. You know, only pull out those trump cards when you have to. Lots of people network tirelessly and build up a massive list of contacts without ever really utilizing it by asking for help, but that's a big mistake because people want to help if they can. It makes them feel good. If you are kind, honest, and appreciative, people will help you if they can unless you abuse their good will.

Networking is essential, and it's not slimy unless you're insincere, devious, or looking to take without giving back in kind. You need to nurture and develop relationships with as many people as you can so that when you need a favor, you can make a phone call and get what you need. Networking is a meticulous, non-stop, give-and-take relationship with people, and it requires real record keeping and organization, constant care, and a great memory. Bottom line: If you refuse to network, your career is over as of right now.

GET IT TOGETHER

It's never too early to start networking. In fact, you're most likely already doing it, just maybe not with a plan in mind. That's the key: Develop a plan and set up a process for recording the vitals on anyone you deem worthy of being a part of your network.

Getting organized doesn't require that much work unless you've been keeping names and numbers of people on the backs of receipts, matchbooks, and Post-it notes. All that's required is some way to keep a list (preferably a database in a spreadsheet application on your computer) of people that you meet. Don't get spooked by terminology—as far as you should be concerned, a database is just another word for address book.

If you've been collecting contact information on a casual, catch-as-catch-can basis, gather it up and consolidate it into a single database. There's no perfect way to do this—scraps of paper get lost or turn into balls of pocket lint in the washing machine, notebook pads get eaten by dogs, laptop hard drives fry when beer is spilled into keyboards—but given the storage space and speed that computers offer, I'd strongly urge you to formalize your networking on a computer and back it up regularly.

That said, do whatever makes you happy. There's nothing wrong with using a spiral-bound notebook, an old Rolodex, or some other means to store this information. Computers are inarguably more efficient, but they do cost a whole lot more. The important thing is to do something—anything.

Once you've decided on a method, set up a spreadsheet (or a document with rows and columns) to record names, job titles, contact information including phone numbers and e-mail addresses, and relevant notes that describe what was discussed in previous conversations. This will become the data pool for your networking. It will keep things organized so that you can actually make use of the information when you need it.

Yes, this sounds rather tedious, but if you structure things this way from the very beginning, it'll make things easier down the road when your network is so large that you simply can't keep it all straight in your head. The goal of networking is to meet as many people as possible who can help you further your career, and if you create the back-office process to manage that information, you'll be positioned to take advantage of the relationships you'll build along the way.

Derek Sivers, CEO/brainchild behind CD Baby, the popular online retail portal for independent bands, agrees. "It's really important to understand that when you're meeting people, there's always going to be more information out there than your brain can handle," he says. "And you need to get comfortable with some kind of database program to keep track of it all.

"Once you've decided on a database to use [like Filemaker, Act, Indie Band Manager, Live Wired Contact, etc.], every person that you enter into it should have keywords associated with their contacts," he says. "Every time you put somebody into your database—your address book—you don't just put their name, address, and phone number in. You put something like 'promoter,' 'lawyer,' 'guitarist,' 'African music,' whatever word you might need to search for in the future, so that over time you develop this incredible resource. It's not that hard. Just have a keyword field and understand how to search for them.

"Whenever I'm having business conversations, I'll put in a little entry saying, 'I talked to them on this day,' so that when you're out there in the whirlwind of promoting your album or touring, and you get a call from someone and you don't remember who they are, you can quickly search your database and recall who they are. And there it is. You can see you already had three conversations with that person. It helps you pick up where you left off."

Sivers recommends that you use your database to keep track of your to-do list so that while you're talking to someone you can enter in a follow-up date on their record that will independently remind you to contact people.

BUILD BRIDGES

Once you've laid the groundwork on the record-keeping system you want to use, it's time to get started building that network. The way you begin is simple. Have conversations with people about what you're doing and exchange contact information with them for future reference. And don't just talk about what *you* do when you're having these conversations. Listen to what other people do, and search for connections.

Discovering existing associations with someone with shared interests is what leads to real relationships, and relationships are the most valuable currency in the music business. The more relationships you have, the better off you'll be when you need to take care of business.

Schmoozing can make you feel self-conscious if you're not being yourself or if it's something that you're not used to doing. One way to keep yourself honest is to make sure you know what you're talking about. Don't talk for talk's sake or to fill up dead air. Talk about what you know, do it from the heart, and don't be pushy about it. There are already enough charlatans in the world. Just be yourself, and that should be good enough for most people.

There are all types in the music business, but the business itself is much more interconnected and incestuous than it appears (I mean that in the best possible way). Talking to people whenever possible is the most effective way to stumble upon invisible connections. Seemingly random exchanges at parties, after gigs, or out on the street can lead to rewarding relationships with people who can offer help that seems heaven sent. It may feel like small talk in the beginning, but it can add up to something much bigger in the long run.

All it takes is for you to establish meaningful familiarity with someone and your network will be off and running. A simple introduction may seem inconsequential at the time, but you never know where that relationship might lead, either tomorrow or years down the road. Maybe that person can't do anything to help you the first time you meet, but they might be able to in the future. The point is that you need to get the word out there, and by talking about what you do and letting people know you exist, you'll slowly build relationships and a reputation. Eventually, over time, you will hit upon the right combination of people who have your interests in mind and will help you get where you want to go.

Jay Rodriguez, a well-known Brooklyn-based sax and flute player in New York's jazz and rock scene, has made a name for himself as a musician, composer, and leader of the popular band Groove Collective—not only for his remarkable talent, but also for his people skills and non-stop networking. This combination of skills helped him land his breakthrough gig as a member of the late salsa queen Celia Cruz's band when he was only nineteen years old, and it's what has kept him a highly sought-after performer throughout the country and around the world.

"My approach is natural because I like people, and I like hearing what they have to say," says Rodriguez. I talk about what I do, find out what other people do, and then I search for the thing that they might need from me and the thing I need from them, or whether they need me at all. You always have to sell yourself, even if it's a casual conversation with someone who may not have any interest in what you do. Understand who they are and what they do for a living, and then once you've told them what you do, figure out if there's anyone they know within the music industry that you'd want to know. Figure out what interests them. You need to find common ground to plant seeds so the business relationship can grow.

"I customize my message to whomever I'm talking with," he explains. "I'll tell them that I'm a part of whatever experience they're into, and it's not a lie. You're not being phony if it's the truth, you're just being really honest about all that you do. It's part of your experience as an artist, and that's what people want to hear. The more you do and the more you commit to, whether a recording or band, the more you can bring forth.

"I'm a musician's musician," says Rodriguez. "A composer, an arranger, a leader, a conceptual artist. There was a time I used to say I could do everything and I'd wing it. I didn't understand that I already had enough experience to *be* it. It was a realization. I became what I already was and learned how to follow through with the responsibilities that came with it. It's a matter of replacing fear with faith. Don't quit before the miracle inside you gets out. Just believe in what you're selling. Spend time on what you need to become, what you will evolve into," he adds. "It takes practice, but you can do it, and people will respect you for it."

Bear in mind that this is all dependent on your willingness to put yourself out there. You've got to have faith in yourself and trust in the karmic potential that a meaningful relationship can sprout up at any point. Yes, bring on the unicorns, rainbows, harps, and crystal amulets full of myrrh and lavender. I admit these last few bits read a lot like a crunchy self-help guide, but you've got to remain open-minded about the possibilities that can occur when you tell people about yourself. If you do you'll make it possible for them to do the same, and then all sorts of wonderful things can happen.

Just be yourself, confident yet humble, and stay open to dialogue and ideas whenever they occur and wherever they come from. You never know when someone who can help you will come into your life. In many cases they might already be in your life, but unaware that they are empowered to help you. For that reason, you need to represent yourself and what you're trying to do with equal amounts of confidence and humility.

The key is to be as good as you can to people, because those same people will always remember it. "Be respectful to everyone, even if you think they don't deserve it," says Joe D'Ambrosio, a talent manager for a roster of well-known producers and artists on the East Coast. "You can't be a phony good guy—you either are one or you're not. Whatever you are will eventually come out when you're networking.

"If you're a brat, you're a brat. If you're good hearted you can thrive as long as you reach out to people and still hold your ground. This is a business where everyone can help each other, but everybody is worried about self-preservation, so you've got to keep at it and believe in the kindness of others." In other words, you never know where it's going to come from or when, so you've got to stay honest and on your toes.

"Everything and everyone is connected," says Jay Rodriguez. "You can travel to a gig halfway around the world and find out that you know someone that someone there knows," he explains. "It's a small world, and that's why it's important to be cool with everyone. Granted, not everybody is going to be on your path, but if you're humble, you'll find brothers and sisters who *are* on your path."

No matter if you're in your hometown or half a world away, the important thing is to follow through on promises and show initiative when you're networking. Musicians, as far as the general population is concerned, are "flakes," so if you can prove that you've got it together, you're starting out with an advantage. If you said you'd send someone your demo, do it today. If you said you'd call or e-mail someone, don't put it off.

Go the extra mile, do whatever is necessary to keep yourself in someone's mind without making a nuisance of yourself. Demonstrate to everyone in your network that you're responsible and that you do what you say. Doing so consistently shows integrity, and it will make their decision to help you that much easier when the time comes.

Look at it in the context of someone who's trying to decide which musicians to hire for a studio session. In most cases, that person will uniformly hire less talented players who are capable enough but who also demonstrate responsibility. No one needs an undependable mercenary. Of course there's a minimum basic standard for ability that everyone has to meet, but once a musician crosses that talent threshold, they have fewer ways to differentiate themselves from the other 500 musicians in the area who can play the same thing. Responsibility and being true to your word are keys that will build your reputation in any network.

TALK IT UP

No matter where you are or what stage of your career you're in, there are innumerable opportunities to network. Don't think that firing off e-mails or calling people on the phone is enough. You've got to get out there and press the flesh. Nobody could ever be accused of doing it too much. Talk to people, get to know them, and look into their eyes. You can't get that type of sincere connection on line or over the phone unless you've already established a relationship with someone.

One of the most productive ways is to do it at your own shows. Meet and greet people before and after a gig. It bridges the physical and emotional gap that exists between the stage and the audience and helps you connect with people on a different level.

Make a point of talking to as many people as you can at your own shows. Not just your friends, but people they bring with them and the people you've never seen before. You know what to expect from people you already know—compliments born out of courtesy and respect—and while taking the time to listen to it may feel good, it isn't typically constructive and can prevent you from meeting other people.

It's important to be creative and proactive, says Rodriguez. "I played a gig at Lincoln Center and was told that certain record-label people were going to be there, so I brought some of my records to give to them. When they didn't show up, I stuck around and gave the records to a radio person I met. The point isn't whether she did something with them or not. It's that you never know what's going to happen or who you'll meet, so you've got to be prepared to act."

It's always a good idea to set aside time to meet new people at your shows, whether by design or spontaneously. Not only are strangers more likely to offer you a fresh, objective perspective on your music, they might also turn out to be a valuable new contact. Of course, it's possible that you'll meet people you don't like or who may rub you the wrong way, but if you find out that someone likes your music without knowing you firsthand, you'll receive a more constructive opinion and enjoy a valuable introduction to someone who can become part of your fan base, as well as a friend.

Going out to see other musicians perform is another effective way to add depth and breadth to your network. And it's so much easier than doing it at your own shows because you can relax—you don't have to worry about dragging your equipment up on stage, performing your set, or breaking down your gear after your set. This means you can show up when it's convenient, watch other bands perform as it suits you, talk to people when you feel like it, and hang out to see what the night brings.

BE SEEN ON THE SCENE

There are two sensible ways to do this: Either go to a club where you've already played (or would like to play), or go support an artist you know (or one you'd like to meet). You could also go to a random club without knowing who's playing, but that's the least effective strategy for meeting people. There's no reason why it can't work, but if you're looking to network there's a much better chance of achieving your goal when you know some of the variables in advance.

There are many benefits that come from networking at a venue where you have performed in the recent past. For starters, you'll probably be recognized at the door and get in for free, and if you were a good tipper when you played, maybe the bartender will hook you up with a free drink or two. Don't think that's trivial: Other people will notice that you're getting V.I.P. treatment and will wonder who you are, and that can't hurt.

But more importantly, by going to a club where you're a known entity, you'll also stand a good chance of running into and/or being seen by people you've previously interacted with—club regulars, other bands, the owners, the soundperson—and whether you strike up a conversation with them or are simply seen by them, that deepens the bond you've already got and puts you in their mind. It lets you talk to a manager at a club and say, "Hey, I'd like a gig here. How about giving me a night?"

If you haven't played at a club enough times for anyone to know your face, it's an opportunity to go out there and sell yourself. Show up with an idea. Figure out what types of acts are being hired on what nights, then drop the name of your band or other bands that you play with. Suggest a group of bands you know that have a similar sound to yours that might draw well if booked together on the same bill.

Start making connections and establish yourself as a part of the local scene. Talk to people who work at the club, talk to people who hang out there, make sure they know who you are so the next time they see you there's something to talk about, even if it's a simple "hello." What matters is that you're seen and heard, because being there in that moment will affect something someone's thinking about in the next moment or the next day.

OFFER YOUR SUPPORT

Opting to support a specific musician you already know and respect deepens your relationship with them simply by showing your face, and they'll probably introduce you to other people who came to see them who may be interested in what you do, as well. And by being in that situation, you initiate situations that could lead to performing on the same bill at an upcoming show, collaborating in some way, or seeing the artist you came to support in the audience at your next gig.

Some musicians struggle with the notion of supporting a contemporary because of competitive feelings, but competition is only in your mind, says Rodriguez. "As you grow up emotionally and spiritually, there's no space or need for that." You may feel like you're competing for the same slots on the same stages in the same clubs—and sometimes you are—but what you're really doing is confronting the same problems and dealing with the same issues. View your support as an opportunity to learn and share with someone who understands what you're going through. And even if their experiences have been different from yours, you can still learn from each other, and you'll also get the chance to see someone else rock the house.

"I recently went out to support a contemporary of mine because I like him," says Rodriguez. "It makes me feel good about music in general when I see other people play, and seeing him tells me who I am. He was so happy to see me there, and it made me feel great. We hadn't spoken in a long time, so we had a long chat after his set. Maybe that brings me work. Maybe that brings me new connections. I can't say for sure, but it definitely brings me perspective.

"This guy is very talented, very well connected, very established, and he has a record deal, so by going to see him play it also gives me the chance to ponder why don't I have things set up the way he does," adds Rodriguez. "Maybe I haven't chosen to go for it the same way, but what's to stop me? Seeing him play helped give me a perspective on where I want to go and where I don't want to go, and speaking with him brought us closer. How can that be bad?"

Going to see musicians you'd like to know is a little bit more of a challenge, especially if they're well known or the size of the venue they're playing at makes face-to-face access difficult, but the rewards can be incredible.

Think about how you feel after a show when you walk out from backstage and make your way through the crowd and someone comes up to tell you how much they liked what they just saw. You're still riding that adrenal high from the performance and the applause, physically spent but emotionally invigorated, but you know damn well you're going to talk to them for a moment, right? Well, of course you are, and there's no reason why you can't be that fan and approach someone *you* admire.

Show up early, maybe during soundcheck, or stick around long after their set, and when you get an opportunity to introduce yourself, make your move. I've met many musicians I really admire this way, and while some of those introductions never went beyond a simple, "Hey, I really like what you do," others led to meaningful relationships with artists who became mentors and friends down the line. If you can make a great contact who later becomes a great friend, you win twice. It's an exponential reward for your effort.

In fact, introducing yourself to someone you admire doesn't have to be the end of it. Why not try to play with the person you admire? If you have access to that person and are reasonably certain that you can keep up with them, there's nothing wrong with asking, whether you're seeking a one-on-one lesson or maybe just offering them an invitation to jam. The best way to improve is to play with people who are better than you, recommends Rodriguez. "You should feel confident about it, not scared. Don't worry about being judged." Teaching and learning are all a part of collaboration, so there's no reason to be afraid that you won't be good enough.

Do the Hang

Playing or associating with other musicians can dramatically expand your network and your fan base at the same time (assuming that your styles are similar enough to appeal to a single crowd). At its most basic level, playing gigs with another band builds camaraderie and leads to gigs and contacts that you might not otherwise get as quickly. And at its most complex, smaller bands benefit from comparisons to larger bands of a similar style and can often ride on the coattails of the more successful bands' success.

"Being associated with other bands was the single most effective thing we ever did," says gONNA gET gOT (a.k.a. G), a Brooklyn-based hip-hop artist whose former band, The O, latched onto a much better-known group through a person who would later become their manager. "One day we walked past a club in New York, and here was this guy ushering us in and telling us to see his band. We started talking to him, we went in, they blew us away and he blew us away.

"From there we started hanging out with him and the band," says G. "They all heard our music and thought it was cool. They were about to get signed, and he came up with a plan to cross promote us on their Website. Whenever someone bought one of their CDs, they received our tape for free. They were a couple of steps ahead of us, and they even helped us fund the cassettes, and it was really effective. By networking with them, we were validated for their fans who might not have ever heard of us. Their ultimate heroes gave us a thumbs up, and that made it okay to like us. We capitalized on their cult, and I'm still seeing kids from back then at my shows today."

Hire Firepower

Another way to network is by working with a band manager or an entertainment lawyer. Neither one would likely tell you that networking on your behalf is part of their job description, but if they're good they probably have extensive, far-reaching contacts and will probably provide you with introductions to people when the timing is right.

Having someone else to toot your horn—a lawyer, publicist, agent—boosts your cachet and prevents you from having to cold-call someone you don't know. That said, don't expect your lawyer or manager to do it. You have to earn it. Good managers and entertainment lawyers are effective not only because of what they know but because of who they know, and they're not going to embarrass themselves or jeopardize a relationship on your behalf until you've shown your value. So it's up to you to give them a reason to believe in you.

Networking can seem like a chore at times, but it's an investment of time and energy that pays more dividends the longer you do it. The key, though, is to develop and use the people skills that will let people know you are generous and sincere. Networking is an emotional and intellectual transaction that should be ongoing over time rather than some random shots in the dark.

Your goal should be to meet people who can help and teach you, and you should leave those same people with a good impression so that they speak highly of you when you're out of earshot. And chances are they will if your intentions are good. If you come off as a sleazeball, people will sense it. Conversely, if you come off like someone who's willing to give without expecting something in return, you're more likely to reap the benefits of someone else's generosity.

KEEP IT REAL

With each relationship you initiate, you'll increase the likelihood of being exposed to someone who can help you when it matters. But to ensure that the karmic wheel turns your way, you've got to comport yourself well when you're building your network. If you're respectful and friendly, you'll be appreciated.

Peter Primamore, a New York-based composer and co-owner of a large music library, eventually built an extremely successful career by networking, but poor people skills kept him toiling in obscurity for years early on. "My arrogance was ridiculous," he says of his many years of playing in bands and Atlantic City lounge acts before truly launching his commercial career by co-writing the theme song to the *Today* show. "I don't know what motivates this arrogance, but I think a lot of musicians suffer from it. We get a little full of ourselves when we know we're good. I knew I was good, but I didn't have the people skills that went with the musical chops; my musical skills were a ten, and my people skills were a four.

"If you have that imbalance, it's highly unlikely that you'll succeed unless you're the mother of all mothers with what you do. Miles Davis didn't need to say 'good morning' to people because he was Miles Davis, but if you're not that great and your people skills aren't what they need to be, you've only got one choice. It's a lot easier to develop the people skills than it is to become as great as Miles Davis."

Musicians feel disproportionately entitled, says Primamore. "Some cats never get over it. They end up being really great players who are really angry." This is important whether you're a session player looking for your next gig or a musician with a small budget asking other musicians to play on a demo. "Anybody that has a couple thousand bucks can hire A-level players for their session, but if you're not at that level of economic stability, you'll have to rely on friends and people you meet," he explains. "And that makes it imperative for musicians to radiate positivity.

"I've played on countless projects for people, and countless people have done favors for me," he says. "But if you're not friendly toward people, no one will do anything for you. And a lot of the time you'll get a better result from someone who really cares about your stuff rather than someone with a mercenary approach. I've had $1,000-a-day guys that come in who are nothing but trouble and guys who play for nothing that give me gold."

Confidence, rather than arrogance, can be an asset assuming you use it appropriately. Primamore once landed a regular piano gig at the Showboat Casino in Atlantic City through ingenious, if not aggressive, networking. "Somehow or other I had gotten the name of the entertainment honcho at Caesar's Palace, and I picked up the employee's house phone in the casino and asked to speak with him. Someone transferred me to his office, he picked up, and as soon as I started talking he asked me how the hell I even got in touch with him. I quickly gave him some funny aside, and he said, 'Okay, come on up and see me. I'll send someone down to bring you up.'

"He seemed so intrigued that I had figured out a way to get to him that he listened to me play," says Primamore. "It happened that I had a nice audition, and he said, 'You're not right for what I do here, but you're perfect for the Showboat [Casino Hotel].' He called his friend, who was the entertainment director at the Showboat, who came over, listened to me play, and gave me the job. Basically, I lucked my way into his network, and with his help I hit the jackpot."

MUSIC CONFERENCES

Music conferences are better known as weeklong parties for the music industry, performing bands, and music fans, but they're the ultimate networking opportunity for everyone involved. Good conferences typically attract hundreds, if not thousands, of like-minded music-business folks to a single, concentrated area over a short period of time. If you have the time and money to spare, you should attend as many as possible. There are always hardcore music fans in attendance to see the wide range of acts that appear from all over the country to perform, and there's also a high concentration of industry players converging on the same town, so you should try to attend at least one major conference a year.

If you do decide to attend a conference, make sure to create a wish list of people you'd like to meet. There are a ton of resources available that'll get you started on figuring out who to contact and how. You can use the guide books from recent music conferences to look for industry types in the directory of registrants, but don't limit yourself to these lists. There are thousands of companies out there with their own Websites. Good places to start include online clearinghouses such as *www.indiemusic.com* and *www.rlabels.com*, industry news sites like *www.billboard.com* and *www.hitsdailydouble.com,* fee-based directories (Pollstar and Galaris are good ones), as well Websites for the major performing-rights associations (BMI, ASCAP, SESAC).

Just about everybody (except for the too-cool people) will be wearing a nametag or some sort of ID badge that says who they are, where they work, and where they live, and if you pay attention to this information it can help you achieve your goals when the right person walks by. No one can memorize the names and faces of mid-level record label executives or cutting-edge producers, but each attendee's badge can tell you a lot in a glance. It may feel awkward, but it's part of the conference ritual, and it'll spare you from selling yourself to people who can't help you and prevent you from blowing off the people who could give you the break you're looking for.

Attending just about any conference will help you build your network, but established conferences like South By South West, MIDEM, and CMJ are much more viable for networking purposes because of their number of attendees and their respective longstanding histories. But no matter what conferences you attend, don't just show up and wing it. You've got to have a strategy for networking or you'll get lost in the haze, hype, and hoopla of panel discussions, showcases, and parties.

Whether you're a conference performer or just an attendee, there'll be endless opportunities to meet other people like you at the conference center and at related activities. But with dozens of events occurring on- and off-site simultaneously, you need to create a prioritized agenda that keeps you focused on enjoying yourself and meeting as many people as you can.

Treat Panels Seriously

Panel discussions are far and away the best—and most structured—opportunity to meet people with your specific interests. The majority of people in attendance show up there because they're interested in the same topic, and most of them are ready to talk about it before, during, and after the discussion. It's essentially an invitation to meet people who are interested in talking shop about the same things you're interested in, so carefully review all the panel topics, circle the ones that sound interesting, and make note of each panel participant's bio so that you can gauge which panels are worth attending and which panelists you should try to meet, if possible.

Arrive early at the room where the discussion is being held, and don't sit in the back—get right up front in the first few rows with all of the attentive people, and make sure you take notes. (At worst you'll learn something and have the notes to fall back on later, and at best you'll have an easy way to refer to follow-up questions for a panelist and an easy way to write down someone's contact information.)

Sitting up front is the best way to strike up conversations with other proactive members of the audience, and it also places you close enough to direct a question to someone on the panel when the moderator invariably opens up the discussion to the floor. And you should ask a question—it shows that you're involved, gets people to notice you, and might motivate other people to introduce themselves to you later on if your question was intelligent and they have something to add.

If you're really interested in the topic or simply want to meet someone on the panel for some other purpose, linger around when the discussion officially ends so that you can approach the person you want to meet with a question, a comment, or even just a handshake. And don't forget to carry around something you can give them—a business card or a CD demo with full contact information—to remind them who you are when you call them on the phone weeks later.

Networking at conference performances and sponsored parties is a little more difficult because the focus is on fun and there's usually a lot of noise and confusion, but that doesn't mean you shouldn't try. Just know beforehand that your success will depend as much on your people skills as it will on dumb luck, but that's how life is in general, so just enjoy the fact that crowds of people who enthusiastically love music as much as you do are in the same place at the same time.

Essentially, by interacting with other people wherever you are, you are networking, and I recommend that you learn to like it. If you can't, at least do a good job of impersonating someone who enjoys it. It's not a membership in the glee-club—just always keep one ear open for conversations about music and take advantage of them. There'll be plenty of time for being a pissy, dismissive rock star once you've actually hit the big time, but until you get there, talk it up, be positive, discuss ideas, and spread the word about your work. You never know when the next schlub you meet at a party will turn out to be the cousin of someone who can help you, and you never know when someone's desire to help the neediest will focus on you. Be yourself, be professional, be interesting, learn how to shut up and listen, and figure out clever ways to connect faces to names—if all else fails, try anagrams or pornographic mnemonic devices.

chapter five

BRANDING YOU

Lots of musicians take an idealistic view of success in the music business, thinking that a focus on anything but music is a waste of time. But if you look at the music business under the harsh light of the capitalist context we live in, keeping your focus on music alone looks like a very bad idea.

Like it or not, music is just another product for sale in the shopping mall of life, and we musicians are simply vendors selling competing brands on very limited shelf space. It doesn't matter if you're selling disposable pop candy or eclectic prog—the brands that succeed are the ones that differentiate themselves from the competition and make people feel good time and again. The ones that don't meet this expectation eventually disappear.

But what's branding, you ask? Well, on the surface it's not that complicated. Historically, branding was the process by which owners of livestock burned a symbol into the skin of their animals with a hot iron to prove ownership. At some point, it became synonymous with stigmatizing (which is perceived to be negative and may explain why so many musicians avoid branding like the plague).

Over time, branding came to mean a reliable process for certifying quality or identifying the manufacturer of a product, and now it has become a complex, multi-billion-dollar business based on the psychology of creating an association between a product, the feeling it gives the consumer, and the company that makes it. Ultimately, branding is about the consumer's emotional allegiance to a product. In your case, branding is about how your fans feel about you.

Your music is a branded product, just like the soda you choose to drink, the clothes you choose to wear, and the soap you use in the shower. You could buy any type of soda, clothing, or soap, but you select specific brands because of their perceived quality, their reputation, and how they make you feel. Lots of these perceptions are based solely on your own experiences using these products, but others come about less obviously, having been insidiously programmed into to your head by the people who make these products. They accomplish this goal via careful messaging and consistent advertising to their target audience.

Some consumers use the same products all the time because they like them. Others use them because they're advertised heavily and that's what they recognize first when shopping. Different people use those same products because they believe in what they stand for, because they think using them makes them cool, and myriad other reasons. No matter what the reason is behind the public's buying decisions, the justification revolves around a branded message that makes the consumer feel good.

Your product is no different than the sodas and soaps of the world. You have a brand, and you need to get the message out there. You must establish a sound, a name, a look, and a philosophy that emotionally resonates with people. Once your brand has developed a consistent reputation, you can leverage it to build an emotional connection and loyalty among the people who are familiar with it. Their loyalty will dictate if they attend your shows and buy your CDs, and it will also influence whether they recommend your brand to others. Your success as a musician is ultimately tied to how many people buy into the branded message you create.

Maybe you never realized that you are a brand. Many musicians don't want to think about it because it contradicts the notion of making music for music's sake and succeeding on nothing but the music's merit. As I've said before, the music business just doesn't work that way. Success comes from having a powerful brand and an effective strategy to market it, not from sticking to some Zen purist ideal and waiting to be discovered.

Musicians everywhere can benefit enormously from serious self-analysis of their brand before they start heavily promoting themselves. Most of us don't want to be bothered or resist doing so because the process (which I'll explain a little later) feels sterile and calculating. I'm not here to tell you that branding is easy—it's hard to create a good brand and get the word out about it, and it's even harder to directly measure its impact. But if you refuse to think about your brand and how to effectively manage it moving forward, you shouldn't ever wonder why you aren't being perceived or appreciated the way you'd like.

Creating a brand strategy and consistently communicating that branded message is critical to your success. You've probably already done this to some extent, perhaps without even knowing that you've been doing it, but even if you've never contemplated any of these issues, don't turn away now—you've got nothing to lose by taking this branding thing seriously. And if you're worried that taking it seriously means you're "selling out," get over it; there's no such thing.

I'm talking about being true to who you are and the music you perform. I'm talking about leveraging your strengths, not undermining your integrity by exploiting yourself simply to succeed. You don't have to become some formulaic pop star with a belly button ring who gyrates and lip syncs to canned music as a way to attract fans.

Effective branding is about being yourself, understanding what you do best, and what it is about you that people like. It's about controlling the way you are perceived, understanding what people like about you, and understanding what else makes those people tick so that you can expand your brand and build an even bigger audience.

Music is more than just a product; it's a visceral, emotional experience, and people will decide if they like it based on how strong their response to it is. People hear music or see it performed live and react to how it makes them feel, but that feeling is dictated by more than just how the music sounds. It's about the message: How do the performers look onstage; how intriguing is the band's logo; is the band wearing jeans and dirty T-shirts or Armani suits; do they have mullets, crew cuts, or purple hair; what types of things do they say between songs or do they not talk at all; how they behave offstage? All of these things, and many more, are part of the branded message.

Brands are social currency among the world's culture, particularly its youth. The brands we choose define who we think we are and imply an unspoken, associated status to everyone who's watching or listening. We align ourselves with those brands we like and those we believe reflect our inner selves. They become signifiers for who we think we are. It's powerful, powerful stuff, and there's no reason why you shouldn't try to harness some of it for yourself.

Large consumer brands like Starbucks, Apple, Range Rover, Nike, and Hennessy have huge brand equity because of the lifestyle they connote, not just the products they represent. People hear or read these names and have immediate emotional responses to them. Is it asking for too much that your brand might someday achieve the same level of household recognition? Perhaps it's a bit out of a reach, but that's not a good reason not to try.

When you create effective branding and consistently deliver its message over time, your target audience will come to believe there is no other band quite like yours. Your brand will come to represent a promise, either unconsciously or overtly, that says, "This is who and what we are, and we will always be this way, if not better. You can count on it."

Take, for example, a McDonald's cheeseburger. They look, taste, and smell the same wherever you go, whether you buy one in Boston, Barcelona, or Beijing. The issue is not whether you like McDonald's hamburgers: The issue is that people have developed trust in the McDonald's brand, and that wasn't an accident. McDonald's managed its branding over decades, and consumers have bought into the promise embedded into it. You should hope that your branding enjoys a fraction of that success.

Think about it: If you are successful at building a strong brand, people will know what to expect when they see your name listed in the local paper or up in lights on the marquee outside a popular venue. There will be no doubt in their minds that you will meet their expectations for a certain type of experience whenever they see you perform. You will become the band they want to see, their standard bearer. They will know that the feeling they first had when they realized *you were it* is the feeling they'll always have when they see you. If that's not success I don't know what is.

Pop culture is the fastest moving business sector there is. One day something's hot, the next day it's not, and as a musician trying to achieve success, you've got to figure out a way to make a mark with your brand and keep it in the minds of enough people so that you can reach the critical mass you desire.

The environment changes rapidly, which makes the need for having a defined brand even more important. A strong brand gives your target audience reassurance and encourages their loyalty, and this holds true whether you're in a bustling metropolis or some rural community. It's especially true for bands trying to make it in a crowded marketplace. A strong brand will help you stand out from all the other alternatives out there.

Obviously you believe something about your music and your band is unique, so your brand needs to say so with its messaging. You must establish an aural, visual, emotional, and culturally meaningful message that consistently identifies, differentiates, and distinguishes you from your local competition. Your brand must transform your music into a wholly unique experience for your audience, intriguing potential fans and keeping existing fans coming back for more.

To start the process of creating your brand, take a step back from your music and assess your band's style or genre for what it is. In other words, who are you? What kind of music do you write and perform? Is it an easily identifiable style and relatively consistent across your entire catalogue, or is it a hodgepodge of various styles that are determined schizophrenically depending on the venue you're playing at? Are you primarily fast and loud, or do you play a lot of soft love ballads? Are you hard rock, dance, pop, hip-hop, or electronica? Death metal, speed punk, emo-core, or country—what's the appropriate code word that'll click with your audience?

Before you can start building a brand, you've got to know what kind of band or artist you are. Once you embark on building your brand, you immediately become an image salesman, and to do so successfully means you've got to know what image you're selling and believe in it, because you can't sell what you can't define.

Your entire band should agree on a description. That doesn't mean dissenting opinions aren't allowed—in fact, I'd encourage them because different views will help you hammer out what you are. Have a meeting with everyone in the band and ask everyone to contribute their opinions. If you can't reach a decision, sit with your band mates and collectively listen to your music, then each of you should write down a list of known bands that you sound most like. (Don't write down those you *want* to sound like, but those you *do* sound like; there's probably a difference.) Look at the list and see if there are any bands in common. If there are, that's a good sign. If there aren't, go down the list and collectively assign a genre or type next to each name. Now look to see if there's one genre that keeps coming up. You should be getting closer at this point.

If you still can't seem to agree, ask people who are familiar with your music but who have nothing at stake (not relatives or a boy/girlfriend of one band member) for their opinions. Do this a few times, and then see if you agree or disagree with the feedback. You might be surprised by what you hear in response, and you should definitely take outsider's opinions as perspectives, not as decrees. If uninvolved people confirm your internal consensus opinion, you've probably arrived at a strong starting place, but if they don't and you still can't come to a unanimous agreement, you need to figure out what, as a group, you are trying to do. What is your focus? Once you've arrived at an opinion in that context, you can start the brand-building process anew. This last bit is a critical step. If you can't agree on what you are, you're probably going to have lots of trouble down the road making other important decisions.

THE NAME GAME

Once you've all agreed on the genre that best fits what you do, the next thing to tackle is your name. Naming a band is one of the most frustrating aspects a band can encounter—why else would there be countless band name generators on line? Should your name be literal or cryptic, literate or crude? Should it have multiple meanings or be something specific? Should it say something about the band or nothing at all? Will people play with the name you give yourself and use it against you in conversation or reviews? Your name should either define who you are and/or what you sound like, or it should be malleable and innocuous enough, like tofu, to absorb whatever meaning or flavor you want it to have in the near future.

This naming process is very subjective, of course, but you need to give it some thought before you act. (Think about peers or young children you know whose parents gave them ridiculous names that doomed the kid to endless taunting and physical torture, like the protagonist in the Johnny Cash song, "A Boy Named Sue.") It's much easier to build a brand with a strong name. A bad name makes it much harder for your brand to stick.

If you already have a name and you've established it over many gigs, you just need to ask yourself whether it is appropriate for the style of music you play. This can be difficult to gauge if you're attached to your name, even if you know it was an unfortunate choice (Hootie and the Blowfish comes to mind). But if you sense deep down that your name doesn't fit, change it now before it's too late. Better to change it now when people don't really know you rather than build up momentum with a name that makes people cringe at the very thought of seeing someone with that name.

The name game is much easier to play if you already know what kind of band you are and what you're going after, but whatever the case may be, keep a few things in mind: Naming your band after a cliché is a huge mistake and one that you'll likely never recover from (at least not from a branding perspective). Full disclosure: I was in a band named after a cliché when I was much, much younger, but there was a reason for it—the name of the band was "One Shot Deal" because we agreed to only play one gig. And we *did* only play one gig, but I've never lived down the name with my oldest friends, and I pity the person who seriously thinks a cliché does them service. It's a bad, unsustainable idea that illustrates a complete lack of thoughtfulness and creativity. Do it at your own risk, and don't ever say I didn't warn you.

If your band has an appointed leader or "frontman," you have the luxury of naming the band after that person (assuming their last name doesn't have too many syllables and is relatively easy to pronounce). It's a very effective way to brand the group and makes it easy for potential fans to identify with who you are and what you're about. The only hitch is deciding whether or not you're a band (Steve Miller Band), an experience (the Jimi Hendrix Experience), an explosion (Jon Spencer Blues Explosion), a group (Edgar Winters Group), or something else entirely.

Many bands choose to keep things more unified and equal, at least from the naming perspective (publishing rights are a different story), and that's probably a good course to take if the person standing center stage has a tongue-twister name. Whatever your decision here, you should be able to justify the name you choose by clearly stating how it reflects what you do or at least coming up with a strong case for it, but if you choose the leader's last name as your default it allows you to opt-out of a tougher decision.

Naming your band after an obscure fact, a piece of art, an inanimate object and a dangling participle, a few words from a famous line of poetry, an intentional malapropism, or some erudite piece of cultural minutia can be an effective way to brand yourself. Doing so creates a sense of intrigue among those who are privy to your insider reference, and they'll be more inclined to like your music because you've established a common bond with them before they've ever heard you play. There will undoubtedly be people who wonder what the name means, but that will serve you well, too, because it gives you something interesting to talk about and lends credence to your image as a deep thinker. Of course, if you pride yourself on being cro-magnon meatheads, your post-doctorate sangfroid won't mesh with your branded message.

Anything that gets people thinking is a good idea in my opinion. If people are intrigued by your name, song titles, or album title, they'll probably give you more credence than some band named "Guns Blazing" or "The Wet Dreams." (If you're currently in a band with one of these names, quit.) Think strategically, think poetically, think linguistically. Come up with a name that says something about who you are or what your music sounds like. Make it memorable, make it evocative, and make it as unique as you are.

IMAGE

Once you've got your sound and your name down, the next thing to consider is·your image. How do you look onstage? Do all of your members wear the same style of clothing, or do you each wear whatever you feel like wearing? Does one guy sport shoulder-length Jheri-curled hair extensions while the other three have spiked Mohawks? Does your lead guitarist play a B.C. Rich Warlock or a Parker Fly while the rhythm guitarist plays a vintage, semi-hollowbody Rickenbacker? How you look speaks volumes to your audience. It's not so much that incongruous clothing, hairstyles, or instruments hurt you so much, but if you can all agree on a single look and stick to it you'll definitely help your cause and you'll also find there are some real advantages to doing so.

For starters, managing your look takes the guesswork out of your pre-show jitters. If everyone agrees that you're a blue-collar band and that your uniform is jeans, boots, and white T-shirts, you don't have to go hunting through the closet for your favorite red velvet shirt and silver lamé pants with the stuffed sock sewn into the crotch and wonder whether you should've worn the seersucker suit instead. Bands that don't have a cohesive look give off the impression that they're a group of individuals rather than a unit. De facto uniforms or styles can be goofy if taken too far (Sixties-style black turtleneck sweaters and berets, for instance, will never be cool again), but if you can share a look and still maintain your individuality your audience will see that you all stand for the same thing. That, in my mind, connotes strength of purpose.

There's probably no better example of this than The Beatles, whose early career was marked by matching haircuts, jackets, drainpipe trousers, and boots (now named after them). The look became part of their brand, and every time their look changed (longer hair, mustaches, beards, less formal clothing) the new look was accepted as an evolution of The Beatles' brand because they did it together.

How you look is a reflection of who you are. When you're part of a group that has the same look, it says a lot about your music. This kind of thinking worked for KISS, the Village People, Devo, Aerosmith, The Cure, and countless others. As long as you're consistent with your brand, you can wear anything you like and still be accepted. Elton John had his outrageous glasses, ZZ-Top has its shag-rug guitars, Marilyn Manson has his androgynous goth-wear, GWAR had its comicbook monster costumes, the divas have their hoootchie-mama outfits. You can choose whatever look you want. Just be consistent.

LOGO

With your identity assured, your sound in place, and your look established, you're ready to come up with a logo. Don't think that you can get away without using one at all—how your name appears says a lot about your brand. Ignoring how your name appears and allowing it to be inconsistently presented only gives off the sense that you are inconsistent and that you don't care. Is that the vibe you want to convey?

Even the most minimalist logo can end up being used in so many ways. Logos turn up on CD artwork, press kits, Websites, T-shirts, stickers you hand out at shows, in local advertising, and maybe on your kick drum. Even if your logo only turns out to be the name of your band in a specific font, it says something about who you are.

Once you've got your logo designed and finalized, make use of it on anything band-related that a potential fan might see. That includes your bio, photos, CDs, Websites, e-mails, flyers, signage, posters, T-shirts, marketing tchotckes, etc. All of these things reflect your brand values, and your logo should be used to consistently project your brand and reinforce it in each one of these instances.

Logos seem simple, at a glance, especially if they're good, and once you have one that works you don't ever have to give it thought again, but coming up with one that stands out and immediately identifies you is extremely difficult. Your logo needs to incorporate the sound, the image, and the focus of your band into a legible but unmistakably artistic message that reinforces who you are and sticks in the minds of your target audience.

Logos can be font-based (nothing but type), image-based (the silhouette of a microphone, for instance), or abstract (like that symbol Prince used to use when he was the artist formerly known as Prince before he became his old funky self again). Ultimately, you want people to look at your logo and get an idea of what you sound like right then and there. If your hallmark characteristic is high volume, the logo should indicate loudness. If your music is speed punk, your logo should imply speed. The logo doesn't need to be over the top, just evocative.

Obviously that's no easy task—there are firms that spend countless weeks and charge massive sums of money to create corporate logos that never accomplish what I've just set out as your goal. But don't get discouraged—it is possible to think creatively and come up with a logo that gets the idea across. The Rolling Stones have perhaps the best one in the biz—you know, the big lips with the tongue sticking out. If you can channel that kind of thinking you'll be fine.

Look at logos used by other bands like yours to start generating ideas. What about their designs works? What can you do to differentiate your logo from all the rest? Don't spend time sketching something that's cool just for cool's sake. Remember, you want your logo to communicate your branded message, not instigate conversations about abstract art.

Having a great idea is one thing, but make sure it's something that can be executed—it's got to be easily reproducible and scalable so that the key details are visible whether the logo appears on a T-shirt or your Website. There's no reason to spend days creating a logo with unbelievable detail when those same details will be lost in reproduction. And whatever you do, avoid those horrific clip-art images found in free software packages—using them stinks like cheap cologne and makes you stand out for the same reasons.

If you happen to know a graphic artist, you might consider asking them to recommend fonts and colors that will work best for your needs. Just don't fall for fashionable color concepts or cutting-edge typographical trends. "The new green" might look great on runway models, but you're a band in need of a logo, not a $7,000 purse. The same goes for high-tech fonts—they might be lauded by art directors at snooty boutique magazines, but your average music fan won't care. Avoid choosing a wacky font that gets you stuck defending something that's unappealing, illegible, or downright unexplainable.

Stick with colors and fonts that are painless to read, simple to reproduce (both on line and in print), and easy to relate to. Stick with a few colors at most (more than two starts to become very expensive to reproduce), and select a timeless font that doesn't require special glasses to be legible.

Follow these rules and you'll come up with a logo design that stands the test of time and doesn't require reinvention or costly rethinking in the years to come.

VENUE SELECTION

Where and when you perform also says something about your brand. Every venue has its own reputation—its brand—and you can easily feed off it or be punished by it. Consider the venues you play at very wisely. Make a point of familiarizing yourself with any new venue you're asked to play at before you agree to perform there. Research what other types of bands play there. Are they like you or completely different? Are they well known or new bands without a fan base to speak of? Is there a built-in crowd that walks into the club off the street, or does the door swing open every time one band's set ends and another begins? Does the venue have a reputation? Is it a hip place where A&R execs drop in for a late night drink, or is it habituated by lushes who are more interested in scratch-off lottery tickets and watching TV? Is the stage big enough and sound system powerful enough to support what you do, or will you be cramped and too loud if and when you perform there?

All of these variables will not only affect how you play but also how your brand is perceived. You might be so happy to be offered a gig—any gig— that you ignore all of these issues and dive right in, and a lot of the time you can do that and get away with it. But when you start playing out regularly, people will begin to draw a correlation between your brand and the places they see you play. You don't want to become associated with dying clubs. You won't be appreciated by whatever crowd is there, and even if you are it's unlikely that it'll matter because you're probably not going to build a buzz playing at the wrong place. You'll be the tree falling in the forest with no one there to hear it. That damages your brand and your self-esteem if it happens often enough.

There's also a fine balance between not playing out enough and playing too much. It's hard to build a local reputation if you don't perform on a somewhat regular basis, but bands that play every weekend run the risk of over-saturating the market with their name and presence, and that puts your brand at risk. If you're not a popular act doing a residency or on tour, clubs will stop booking you if you play too often—bands without a certifiable "buzz" that overbook themselves have trouble drawing crowds on a consistent basis, and that's a bad trend to initiate. It's far from appealing to club owners and talent buyers, and fans who notice that you're playing every week but aren't being written about in the local papers will dismiss you as nothing special.

YOUR AUDIENCE

Understanding your current audience is key to creating and managing a compelling and effective brand, and it'll also help you expand your brand to attract an even wider audience. Do you have any idea what it is that your current fans like about you? Instead of guessing or hoping it's the aspect that you'd like it to be, ask them. As always, take what an individual might say with a grain of salt—it could be overly glowing or harsh—but take notes and try to get an overview.

The idea here is to accentuate the positive aspects of your brand that they are responding to and to minimize or eliminate the things they collectively don't like or don't respond to. (That is, unless those are the very characteristics that you think are working for you, in which case you should do some careful self-examination.)

Find out what the deal is from the crowd's perspective. Think of it as conducting a marketing focus group. Ask specific questions to learn what they think of your product. For example, do they like your overall sound but wish that they could hear the lyrics more clearly? Well, maybe you're playing too loud for the singer to be heard. Then again, maybe your singer should enunciate more, or perhaps you're just playing in clubs where the soundman isn't mixing you correctly or the P.A. is inadequate. You can change that by turning down or playing someplace that can support your sound.

But don't stop when you've gotten an earful about yourself. The *really* important stuff is finding out about what else they like. You ultimately want a large audience that can only be defined by paying customers, but chances are you're not there yet. It's more likely that you've got a pretty specific fan base, and that definition can provide you with valuable information about how you're doing and how you can improve.

Get out into the crowd and find out what they think of your band. Listen to the language they use to describe you—and listen closely to the words they use to describe your music so that you can use them in your branding message. Find out what other bands they like, then try to figure out what those bands are doing well and what characteristics you share in common with them.

What do your fans look like, generally speaking? Are they thrift-shop types, surfer punks, clean-cut 9-to-5ers, big-haired mall rats, or an even mix? What types of clothing do they buy, and where do they shop for it? How old are they? Do they only go to certain clubs when they go out, or will they go anywhere to see you play?

Once you know the answers to questions like these, you can refine your brand message and refocus your marketing efforts so that your brand resonates more clearly with your existing fan base and becomes known by more and more people who would like it if they knew about it. Having said that, there's a difference between expanding and extending your brand, and it's important to be very wary of doing too much of the latter. There's nothing wrong with trying to gain a larger market share (e.g., more fans in a wider geographical region), but you don't want to weaken the brand to do so.

Don't stretch your brand. Dance with the one you came with. Stick to your core competencies. Accentuate the very things that made you appealing to people in the first place. Sure, there's no reason why you can't evolve—in fact, you'd better be able to—but if people are already responding to your music, you don't need to change genres midstream. Don't integrate a scratch DJ into your sound because it's what everyone else is doing. Nobody will fall for the me-too approach, and you'll diminish your brand by doing it. Stick to what works and follow your creative muse without messing with what you've already built.

As I just mentioned, you've got to be willing and able to evolve over time. The strongest brands make adjustments without losing any of the integrity that they've already established. Sure, some bands make bad albums or bad choices, but often they have cemented their brand so well in the public's consciousness that they can recapture the magic and remain successful.

The band U2 is a great example of this. Their career has spanned decades, and while they tweaked their style a few times, they've never turned their backs on their core strength. No one can honestly say that they don't know what to expect from U2 when they hear their name mentioned in conversation or see it up in lights.

They have managed to stay fresh while remaining true to their core competencies. They've evolved without stretching their brand too much. They still exude passion, they still command respect, and their new music hasn't alienated their early adopters. They keep building their fan base, album after album, year after year, and the brand only gets stronger and more defined. Their image is unshakeable, their sound is often imitated but immediately identifiable when it's the real thing, and they always stay on message. They satisfy a need and fulfill a promise they started making well over thirty years ago. Follow their lead and take control of your brand right now. It'll take a lot of work, but if you build the brand and deliver its message consistently, the fans will come.

chapter six

YOUR PRESS KIT

To be a success in the music business, you have to publicize, promote, or market yourself to a broad audience, but you can't accomplish this without a press kit. It is the minimum basic requirement needed to even contemplate success in this business. It is your calling card to the industry, and without it you only exist off the radar screen, floating in space, powerless to attract the attention you crave and the respect you deserve.

The average press kit includes a CD, a band biography, a reproducible photograph, and at least one reprinted example of media coverage your band has received, preferably from a reputable media source. The entire package is used to introduce people who don't know much (or anything) about you to your band and its music.

Press kits are the industry standard for presenting yourself, and anything less is inappropriate unless you've been specifically instructed to forego the formality. You may not like it, but it's a fact of life, just like wearing a tuxedo to a high-school prom—if you want to go to the Big Dance, that's what you're supposed to wear. It can be white, it can be black, it can be blue, but it better be a tuxedo, and it better fit or you're going to look like an idiot. Want to go without pants? Save that for after the prom....

Sure, there are instances where your music alone will be sufficient to impress a specific person, but that usually happens when you're already a known entity in the business with an established following and professional representation. Things typically don't work that way for small, unknown bands, and you shouldn't try to be the one to break the mold.

Putting together a press kit is easier than you might think, but it does take some effort. To start, break down the press kit's individual components on a master list or document, then create a checklist beneath each component with descriptions of what you need to accomplish, which band member will take care of each task, and what the deadline is. Address this master document on a regular basis until you have completed it, and then you'll be ready to put your press kit to work.

THE CORE COMPONENTS

There are four essential components that must be included in your kit: Your music, your bio, your photo, and at least one reprinted press clipping about your band from a newspaper, magazine, or Website. (This last component may be the hardest one to come by, but I'll address that later. For now, just put it on your list.)

Your Music

The most important component of all is obviously your music. Whether it's your first demo or your fourth album, your music is the reason the press kit exists in the first place, and everything else is there to support it. Until you have a finished demo or album in hand, you don't need any of the other components and shouldn't even consider them until your CD is mastered and on its way to the reproduction house.

Today's technology allows virtually anyone to record a pretty impressive-sounding album at home—at least in theory—so there's really no excuse for not having a near-professional quality recording of your best music that you can shop around. That's the point, isn't it? Your goal is for people to want your music, whether that person is a fan in a music store or a talent buyer at a popular music venue you'd like to perform at, and there's no better way to accomplish that goal than to have a CD that sounds great.

Earlier in the book I discussed how to make a demo, so I'm not going to get into that here. But making your music available in a presentable form (a three-song demo to send to clubs, a best-of compilation that you burn specifically for program managers and A&R executives, or the pre-release version of your latest album) is an absolute necessity. Whatever you do, make sure your CD is mixed to sound great and make sure it's mastered so that there aren't any unintentional changes in volume or timbre. I know, this should be obvious, but you'd be surprised how many bands can't manage this. These are necessary actions; failing to do either one is a huge mistake.

The most convenient and presentable format you could choose as a vehicle for your music is a CD. You can supplement your CD with downloadable mp3s of non-album (or non-demo) tracks on your Website, but consider that a secondary strategy to support the music included in your press kit. If you can't afford the cost of CDs, cassettes are still a passable alternative, but their fidelity is poor and they're far less convenient than CDs at this point. Vinyl is an expensive alternative unless you're a DJ; any other format is passé or obscure and should be avoided.

While the music and its recorded quality may be the main focus of your press kit, you can't just take a freshly burned CD-R out of your computer, scrawl your band's name onto it, slap it into an empty jewel box, and send it off to a record company. No, the product needs specific information on its packaging.

If you've already gone through the hard work of creating a CD with artwork that you intend to sell, you've probably considered a lot of what I'm about to say, but even if you've already jumped through those hoops, you need to make sure your packaging covers all the important bases.

For starters, the name of your band and your band's critical contact information (name and phone number of the band's management or primary spokesperson, a band-related e-mail address, band Website URL) must be clearly printed not only on the CD itself but on the inside cover art and the back panel, as well. You want the person who's listening to your CD to know how to get in contact with you if they misplace the CD or the jewel box, and if you don't have that information in all of these places you might end up missing out on the opportunity you hoped for.

A common mistake many bands make is forgetting to include the name of their band and the name of their record on the "spine" of their cover art (the narrow, hinged, side portion of the CD jewel box). This is critical because CDs piled on someone's desk all look the same from the side except for the information on the spine. The spine is the only spot that clearly identifies it from all the others until the person pulls it out and gives it a listen. Don't even think about omitting this information. It seems like a small detail, but it's one that you can't afford to bypass.

Although costs have come down over time, it's still not cheap to buy large quantities of CDs, whether you're going to burn them yourself or if you're buying them from a professional reproduction house. Inevitably you'll be given the opportunity to save a little money by purchasing CDs in slimline jewel boxes. The cases are narrower than standard jewel boxes, which I guess is good for storage purposes, but not for yours. They don't have space for you to put contact info on the spine, which means they get lost in stacks of CDs. And furthermore, they just look cheap. Being frugal is important, but don't do it here.

You'll learn this the hard way if you ever call a club to find out if the talent buyer has listened to your CD. If they haven't, your call is probably going to be the last good chance you have of influencing them to do so. If they're up to it, they'll likely hunt for it while you're still on the phone, but you're going to be out of luck if that information isn't on the spine for them to see. If they can't find your CD within a few minutes, it won't be seen again until it ends up in a used CD store or next to a half-eaten hotdog in a garbage dump (most likely the latter, I'm afraid).

Aside from the basic contact information on the CD, the artwork, and along the spine, everything else is gravy. Sure, great artwork might make someone more inclined to pick up the CD if they've got time to care, but who's to say what will work and what won't? You're better off sticking with the key information on a plain white paper insert and leaving it at that unless you're sending out finished copies of your album, in which case you should pursue whatever artistic course you desire and/or your budget allows. (You can always let the recipient know that you'll send them the finished artwork if they need or want it.)

One last detail you should consider using on your CDs is a UPC bar code. A UPC code—short for Universal Product Code—is the machine-readable bar code scanned at retail registers. The code consists of a 12-digit number, as well as bars that represent the number's graphical equivalent. The first six digits refer to a manufacturer's identification number, the next five digits represent the item number, and the last digit—called a check digit—enables the scanning device to determine if the rest of the number was scanned correctly. A UPC bar code on your packaging gives you the ability to accurately track your sales, which is beneficial for lots of obvious reasons. In the context of your press kit, it shows those in the know how serious you are about what you're doing and enables them to verify how many CDs you've sold in a specific geographical region, giving you immediate credibility if the sales numbers are impressive. Look at it this way: If you plan on being around for a few albums, get yourself a UPC code now and start using it on all your records. Many people get them and never need them, but you don't want to be in the position of wishing you had one when it's too late.

Many CD production houses have their own code and will let you use it for free or a small fee if you ask them, but you can also obtain your own. For more information about UPC codes, call or write to the Uniform Code Council at (937) 435-3870; info@uc-council.org.

The Band Bio

Once you've got your CD ready to go, it's time to turn your attention to the bio. In my experience, the bio is the most labor-intensive component to finalize after the music because it's something you and your band mates have to create out of thin air, and it requires constant tweaks, modifications, and rewrites as you progress through your career and your story grows and changes.

Your bio is essentially the story you want to tell about your band and your music. It's not a biography in the book sense. It's a brief summary of who you are, what your music sounds like, your underlying branded message, and why the person reading it should care. Don't make it more than it needs to be.

Since the music is the primary focus of the press kit, create a bio that supports the music and tells its backstory without requiring too much concentration from the reader. Most bios will be read while the first track of your CD plays in the background, so you've got to keep it informative and colorful without getting too deep into philosophy or veering off on esoteric tangents.

According to veteran publicist Steve Karas, senior vice president of publicity and video at Windup Records, a band's bio should be clear and to the point so that it provides the journalist, radio person, booking agent, talent buyer, or retailer at the receiving end a clear vision of the project and the artist. "Bios should be short, preferably one side of a single page," he says. "They should never be verbose just to be verbose. Be descriptive and intelligent without being too intellectual or over the top." (Don't shrink your type below 10 points to squeeze in extra text or it'll be too hard to read.)

Karen Wiessen, senior director of media and artist relations at Island/Def Jam Recordings, agrees with Karas' assessment, noting that most bios she has seen during her career have typically been long, droning, and boring. "A million publicists say the same thing about music, but most folks don't have time to even read the bio," she says. "Just make your bio interesting. Keep it short, one to two pages, just the basic facts. If you've got some sort of history you can get away with two pages, but there's got to be something genuinely interesting about the band in there."

Musicians aren't necessarily writers, so it's no surprise that penning a good bio is tough. But don't fall prey to using antiquated or formal sounding language, says Aleba Gartner, owner of independent public relations firm Aleba Gartner Associates. "Bios often sound forced and unnatural because the bands are trying too hard to be something they're not. They use language that is very corporate sounding, and they're often really generic, uninteresting, and have nothing to do with the band," she says. "The bio is not some institutional development project—you're not asking donors for money. That's what corporate language is for. In your bio, you want to humanize whoever you are. Flesh out your bio with personality, not grand statements that are ultimately empty. Try a little detail, or some humor. But avoid being cutesy or in-your-face hip. That can backfire."

Some bands and publicists concoct bizarre stories to catch the interest of jaded journalists and bored booking agents, which is a pretty good idea if you're a skilled writer and/or the story you decide to tell is captivating. But you've got to be honest with yourself about whether this approach serves your band better than a straightforward bio will. Think long and hard about the impression you want to make before you start writing.

Wiessen suggests that it's good for young bands without much history to approach their bio from a less traditional angle. "The bio doesn't have to be two sides of a page with nothing but the facts. Have a little fun with it, be a little off-the-wall, a little irreverent," she says. "If you do it well you'll probably get noticed faster than if you were trying to play it straight like a major label would." That might mean creating an alter-ego protagonist, or maybe a larger than life persona that's a little off beat, perhaps a little bit out there. Whatever you do, make your bio colorful, and make sure the presentation works on a test audience before you send it out.

With that in mind, I've read band bios that were very entertaining if you're a fan of creative writing or Raymond Chandler mystery novels, but all that writing talent was misplaced because there wasn't a correlation or connection between the tone of the bio and the band's music. Make sure there's some stylistic consistency between them, particularly when you take the non-traditional route.

And stay away from non-musical and political issues unless that's what your band is all about. You can quickly turn off or lose a reader with incessant politicizing. Make short mention of your political stances or beliefs then let the music do the talking (unless, of course, you're sending your bio to someone who's officially involved in a political movement or a grassroots organization that you support). Leaning on a trendy political issue for effect without backing it up in your music implies that you're a poseur. It might be the truth, or it could be just a misperception, but either way it doesn't help you achieve your goal.

Some publicists try to capture a reader's attention by sending out photocopies of handwritten notes, but to me that's self-defeating because the personal touch of someone's scrawl is ruined by the impersonal act of photocopying. All that says is you wanted the reader to think you cared enough to write to them specifically but you were too lazy to really do it. If you want to write a personal note, do it—it's a great idea if you want someone to know something specific that's not included in your standard bio, but otherwise stay away from photocopying handwritten notes. Fact is, these days most people's handwriting looks like hieroglyphics, and most people would rather read something that's typed. Save the old-world charm for letters to grandma.

One publicist tactic that works well is to compose a bio in the form of a question-and-answer interview. Come up with questions that someone should ask you, as if you were being interviewed on TV or in *People* magazine, and answer the questions as clearly and creatively as you can. You're not trying to fool the reader into thinking you were interviewed; you're simply answering the basic questions they'd expect to see in your bio but in a different way, providing them with colorful insights and interesting aspects of your band in a more conversational tone.

Finger Eleven, one of the bands that Karas works with at Windup Records, chose the Q&A format as the bio for their third record. "Rather than doing a traditional bio, they created two different sheets that were serviced with the record. One was eleven questions about their past, and the other was eleven questions about the actual album that was released," he says. "Both were more focused on information, offering clarity without editorializing. Questions in the Q&A, factoid-type format definitely give people who don't know the band a very solid introduction in a succinct way."

This type of approach streamlines the process by preventing you from going off on unnecessary tangents or what amounts to patting yourself on the back with a glowing record review. If the reader isn't interested in the question, they'll move onto the next one. Just be yourself, be interesting, and tell it like it is.

Boastful claims ("we're redefining rock 'n' roll") and hyperbole ("it is the sound of hell unleashed") are transparent attempts to seem better or more important than you are—don't bother. Using tired clichés and verbicidal bombast will send the wrong signal to anyone who hears your music unless you're being ironic or self-deprecating. Regardless of the intent, it's far better to let the reader come to their own conclusion when they listen. That's far more exciting than being hit over the head with claims like, "we are the best band ever." Let your listeners figure it out themselves—that kind of joyous discovery fuels the kind of passion and interest that'll make you a star.

Ultimately you should write a bio that feels right to you, but if you've never written a bio before, it's probably best to stick with a traditional format that's straight and to the point. That's especially true if the person writing the bio isn't part of your band organization and doesn't have much experience writing them. Make sure to discuss the style you want them to use. You don't want any surprises.

If you're taking the traditional route, start by creating an outline that you can use to address the major points you want to convey:

1. Include your band name and all of your contact information on the top or bottom of the release—this includes your primary contact's phone number and e-mail address, as well as the URL for your band's Website. Don't worry about formatting the document yet. Just make sure the correct info is there before you start typing anything else.

2. Has anyone famous said something positive about you? If so, place it up above the main text of your bio inside quotation marks and make sure to attribute each blurb to the person or publication it appeared in. Take advantage of someone else's credibility if they say something nice about you.

3. Who are you? What is your band's name? What kind (genre) of band are you? Introduce yourself and your sound in one strong, descriptive but uncomplicated sentence, two at most.

4. Discuss the music that this bio supports. What does it sound like? Is it your first record? Your fourth? Was it produced by a known entity with a reputation to speak of, or did you record it yourself? Did anything out of the ordinary happen while you were recording it? Weave a relevant but interesting story, and avoid clichés.

5. Name some musical influences or points of reference that the reader will know and respond to—not your typical "tastes like chicken" stuff, but actual names of bands and artists you care about and styles of music.

6. What have you done in your career that sets you apart from all the other bands whose press kits arrived on the same day as yours? Why should the reader take note?

7. Have you had any notable successes? Have you performed with any well-known artists? Gone on any recognizable tours? Has any of your music been played more than once on a college or commercial radio station? Have you performed at any music conventions or been covered by a reputable magazine or Website? Have you won any prizes? Don't leave out any juicy bits.

8. What's your band's vision? Why is your latest record important? Condense everything in this outline into a powerful closing statement about your band. It should be an overarching mission statement that says what the reader should expect from your record and/or your band in the near future.

The outline above is standard fare, but you don't need to follow it to the letter. Try to address each point, and if that doesn't work, tackle the parts that are easiest to answer, making sure to give the reader a clear sense of who you are, what you sound like, and what your vision is. The rest is gravy.

If you can keep to this sort of outline and manage to fit it all on one page, you'll probably have a great first draft. It's a "first draft" because you need to have someone with a clue edit it for grammar, spelling, and punctuation. Once you make the necessary changes and adjustments, make sure everyone else in the band is satisfied with the finished product.

If you're not completely satisfied, visit some major-label Websites and read the bios of artists on their roster, particularly newer ones that you're not that familiar with. Get accustomed to the phrases used and the language, focus on what the publicists who wrote them are trying to communicate, then come up with your own unique ways to describe what you do. Copy a format you like and paraphrase the original filler copy and plug in the stuff about you that's special. Look at other bios to make sure you're not leaving out anything critical. No one is expecting you to be a brilliant wordsmith, but you should be able to put together a short essay about yourself if you follow these guidelines.

Once you're satisfied that you've got good copy, it's time to format it. How bios appear on the page is primarily dictated by the style of bio you choose to write. The standard bio typically appears with the text flush-left (meaning each successive line of text starts along the same vertical axis on the paper) with either a ragged or justified edge. (Ragged type has lines of naturally spaced words that end wherever the last letter of the last word falls, while justified type—like that of this book—has lines of text that are all the same length.)

Your band name or logo should be placed at the very top of your bio in a headline-style using bold text. If you're citing quotations that have been made about your music by people with star-power, place them immediately beneath the headline and use a bold or italic typestyle to call attention to them. You can also weave them into the bio itself, but if the person is well known you'll be better served by getting their comments noticed as quickly as possible.

The body text of the bio should be broken into short paragraphs, and there should be a few extra line spaces, if possible, between the last line of text and your primary contact information, which goes along the very bottom of the page. If you choose a non-traditional style for your bio, you might as well do the same with the way your format it on the page. Just don't make it one long paragraph.

Here's an example of a bio for perhaps the world's greatest unknown act—my band.

FULLER
Breaking New Ground With Fourth Release

Forged in the basement of a former sweatshop on New York's Lower East Side during 1999, the cinematic sound of Fuller is complex, dramatic, muscular, and proudly vocal-free. The group taps into both the sonic aggression of rock and the exploratory aesthetics of jazz, with tightly orchestrated music that boasts a wide dynamic range and a strong sense of melody. "Propulsive, smart and snappy, quick, quirky and quiescent...like bathing in a new sea of sonic possibilities...bath change, Fuller. Fuller, Fuller," says Gary Lucas, esteemed guitarist for Jeff Buckley, Captain Beefheart, and Gods & Monsters.

If the names Mac Randall, Michael Gelfand, and Peter Catapano sound familiar, that's because you've seen their bylines in publications like the *New York Times, Rolling Stone, Esquire, Musician, Salon,* and *Launch*. As Fuller, they have performed at NYC clubs such as Mercury Lounge, Knitting Factory, Southpaw, and Tonic, as well as Boston's Lizard Lounge and as part of the '03 SXSW conference.

In 2000, Fuller recorded an EP called *The Tiers Suite* (named for Wharton Tiers, longtime Sonic Youth soundman and friend of Fuller). Four separate pieces linked by interlocking themes, *The Tiers Suite* ranges from pastoral folk-jazz to paint-peeling avant-rock. Parts of the EP are featured in the indie-film soundtracks of Nyle Garcia's *Humidity* and Jane Gaffney's *Cowboy*.

February 2002 marked the completion of Fuller's first album, *Year of the Rat*. All eleven tracks were recorded and mixed in the converted Chinatown basement that also served as the band's rehearsal space. Water leaks, ceiling cave-ins, and a biblical rat infestation plagued the recording process, but the kaleidoscopic prog of "Privy To The Math" and "Karmic Overhead" and the dreamy soundscapes of "Peekaboo" and "Elephant Rock" prove the band's resolve was worth the effort.

Fuller followed up with a five-song EP called *The Lotus* in October of 2002. Recorded, mixed, and mastered by Wharton Tiers at his Fun City Studio over a two-day period, the condensed sonic burst perfectly captures the band's masterful control of chaos. From the implosive introspection of the title track and angular thwack of "Daisy Cutter" to the sauntering Steely Dan swank of "Catman Shuffle" and Appalachia-cum-Apocalypse groove of "Veronsky," *The Lotus* captures the band pushing against the mainstream as it boldly expands its musical vocabulary.

Fuller's newest record, a majestic, twelve-song tour de force tentatively titled *38*, further reveals the band's penchant for stretching aural waistlines and represents the band's most mature and complete effort to date. Look for it in stores and on line—or in your mailbox—in August of 2005.

For booking and interviews, call 212.555.1212 or e-mail fuller@fuller-nyc.com

Band Photos

Up until about a decade ago, there was a lot of importance placed on the venerable 8 x 10, black-and-white glossy photo and its place in your press kit. But today, with Internet access virtually ubiquitous, it's debatable whether a photo of any kind at all is needed in your press kit. From a traditional perspective, the photo has always been part of the finished package. Even today, a photo is needed if you're lucky enough to have a magazine editor review your record or decide to run a feature story on you, but any art director will tell you that they'd rather download a high-resolution image from your Website than work with a photo you send them in your kit. So why bother?

Realistically speaking, nobody really needs to see your photo in the press kit, but it's still a nice touch if you don't mind the expense and want to make one available. Magazine writers and people booking gigs at clubs will be able to make a deeper assessment of you based on how you look in your photo, and I suppose an A&R person might do the same if they bother to look at your press kit at all.

In all cases the person receiving your kit is going to be interested in your music first and foremost. If they're still interested after hearing your music and reading your bio, the photo could go one step further toward confirming that you fit what they're looking for.

That said, coming up with a band photo the old fashioned way is going to cost you a lot of money that you really don't need to spend, even if someone else is paying for it. Good photographers are hard to find, and they charge high rates for their experience, expertise, and equipment (cameras, lenses, lights, studio time, and assistants cost beaucoup bucks these days). Film isn't cheap, either, and developing the film just to see what all the shots look like will cost you a pretty penny.

If you go the old school route, you'll pay to reproduce your photo, you'll pay extra to include your logo and contact information on that photo, and you'll pay a premium unless you order up a large print run. Before you know it, your band photo will end up costing a month's worth of gas on a tour. If they're using digital equipment, you'll save somewhat on film costs, but you will be charged for the time they have to spend on the back-end processes. Not to take anything away from professional photographers, but in this day and age you're better off saving up for the gas money.

Instead, ask a friend with a digital point-and-shoot camera to take your photo. The photos can be taken virtually anywhere and anytime you like, either outdoors or inside, and without having to worry about how much the film will cost. You'll be able to look at the photos right away on the camera's LCD screen or on a computer monitor, and you'll be able to edit them, if need be, without incurring any costs, assuming you know someone who's reasonably skilled with photo-editing software. Most junior high-school students can handle this task, so don't worry if you're not that skilled yourself. In the worst-case scenario you can surely find some starving college student to tweak your digital photos for next to nothing. That or pay your niece or nephew five bucks; it'll be worth it.

Once you've decided on a particular photo to use and have edited it accordingly, you have to superimpose your band name, contact info, and logo in the margin. (Yes, it's that damn branding again.) Once you've done all this, print out as many as you need on photographic paper at home or at a place like Kinko's. Keep in mind that the paper and toner cartridges aren't going to be cheap, so you might want to consider taking it to a professional printer if you need more than a handful at a time—pros are usually better equipped and more precise when it comes to handling big jobs, and they will make it cost-effective for you if the job is truly worth doing on their end. And even if you can't get around the high cost of reproducing your photos, you saved a great deal by tackling all the other steps yourself.

Conceptually, your photo should convey whatever ideas you think best represent your band. There's no need to be deadly serious, with scowls or dour looks, unless that's the image you want to project. Silly costumes, fake fangs and blood, and colored contact lenses aren't necessary unless you wear them onstage or want to look like a cartoon character. Instead, just be who you are, and try lots of different looks and environments until you get something that strikes the right chord with the entire band. Remember, you're probably not going to want to go through this process again for a while, so do your best to get a photo everyone can live with.

It's said that a picture is worth a thousand words, so yours ought to be good for a few hundred, don't you think? Say something with your photo. Don't be lazy and stand around in a semi-circle like a posse of goateed thugs with your arms folded looking like you might just be bad enough to steal someone's lunch money—that photo has been done thousands of times, and it's sucked in each and every instance. Your photo should represent your brand and what your music sounds like. Don't be typical.

If posed shots feel too self-conscious, have someone take photos of your band in action onstage during a gig. If regular street clothes feel too ordinary, try dressing up in matching suits or clothes that personify your brand better than your uptight work clothes. If you think your features look too dull, spruce up your look with a little eyeliner or some hair product. Be creative, be spontaneous, and don't fall prey to self-consciousness. Walk the streets looking for inspiring locations, interesting backgrounds, or "found art" props that'll make people notice that there's something different about the way your group looks. Most importantly, relax and remember to smile at the birdie.

Press Clippings

Nobody will believe you if you say you're the greatest thing since sliced bread, but you can bet that millions of folks will believe it if they see it on the cover of *Entertainment Weekly*. You want to collect as many press clippings as possible, but unfortunately they're the one press kit component you can't legitimately create on your own. Getting that first one is tough because it's hard to convince someone to write about you when you're unknown. It's only after you've reached critical mass and there's a buzz around you that people start to care and decide they want to chime in with their opinions.

Having at least one article that's been written about you, whether it's from a local free newspaper or the *New York Times*, can make a huge difference in how people perceive you. Most people are easily swayed by the opinions of others, and if someone "important" took the time to pay attention to your music and write about it, then it must have some significance and be deserving of their attention. When it appears in your press kit, the person who sees it will take notice and immediately give a nod of credibility, even if it's just a small clipping. Anything's better than nothing.

That kind of credibility is a little superficial, I suppose, but it's directly proportional to the perceived authority or clout of the person who wrote the piece, the reputation of the publication it appeared in, and the respect that the person reading it might have for that writer or publication. Early on, the prestige of one writer or publication over another one doesn't really matter. The point is to get the ball rolling. A press clipping about your band in a local high-school newspaper is better than not having that same clipping, and you've got to start somewhere. You can stop using it when *Rolling Stone* gives you 3½ stars in their review section, but until then, it'll have to do.

Keep in mind that the music industry in general is infamous for its failure to pay attention to talent until someone else discovers it. No one wants to make a decision until some tastemaker deems it hip, and then all of the sudden everyone is on it like flies. Take comfort in the fact that when someone in the press feels strongly enough about your music to offer their opinion in a public forum and sign their name to it, everyone else will join the chorus, and from there lots of things can start to take off for you. So what you need to do is get one press clipping—just one—to get that buzz happening, and it's really not that hard if you set your mind to it.

How to Get Press Clippings

To get yourself covered in a publication, you'll need to send out your existing press kit components, along with a pitch letter to local editors who might be willing to review your record or possibly write a live review of an upcoming performance. Yes, I know, it's a Catch-22, but that's how it works.

If you enjoy the act of banging your head against a wall, you can start at the top of the food chain and take your chances by sending kits to specific editors at *Mojo, Spin, Revolver, Esquire,* or any other large consumer publication that covers popular culture and entertainment. Just be realistic about your chances.

Editors at major publications receive hundreds of press kits a month from established labels that they rarely get to listen to, and the odds of them opening your package and playing your CD instead of one of those from a known entity are just barely better than winning the lottery. It doesn't mean you shouldn't try your luck, but don't count on hitting the jackpot.

You're better off starting with smaller publications and working your way up to the big guns once you've tasted some success. You should already be familiar with all the local newspapers, niche publications, and 'zines that cover your type of music, so take some time to gather them altogether and study the masthead and bylines for names of writers and editors who have written pieces about bands like yours. The Internet also provides opportunities for coverage. Go on line and seek out publications and e-commerce portals that run reviews of independent acts, like *www.cdbaby, www.jamband.com,* or one of many e-zines that you can find with a simple online search.

On many sites users/listeners/buyers can submit their own reviews of records, which means that you can make up an alias or ask your friends to write glowing reviews of your band. Hey, that's what professional writers do on Amazon's book site to get on the *New York Times* bestseller list, so why shouldn't you?

Don't stop with music-related publications. Non-music media outlets might be interested in you if there's something about you that would interest them. Maybe there's some technology or education angle you can work your way into, or perhaps a business story. Maybe there's some "metro" or "city story" worth covering. It's up to you to figure out a clever way to get your band covered, then determine who the right person is to contact and sell them the idea.

You shouldn't limit your editorial research to staff writers. If you read the music press enough, you'll start to familiarize yourself with the names of writers who appear in numerous publications. They are freelancers, working as hired guns for anyone who'll pay them, and they, more than anyone, can be your greatest boosters if they like what you're doing. When they find a band they really like, they'll pitch magazines and newspapers all over the country until they find someone who's willing to publish their piece—they usually know the staff editors better than you do, they're better at pitching articles than you are, and they'll do a lot of your work for you. In the end you'll end up with something you can use in your press kit, and you'll have hardly lifted a finger. Good deal, eh?

Professional publicists voraciously read daily newspapers, weeklies, and monthly magazines for just this reason. They understand how the news gets covered, they familiarize themselves with all the staff editors and freelance writers, they come up with story ideas, and they constantly dream up ways to publicize their clients and get them media coverage.

Treat yourself as your own client and do exactly the same. Read trade magazines like *Billboard* and specialist publications like *EQ* or *Pro Sound News*. And read non-music publications like *Smithsonian, Boy's Life, Gourmet, and Bride's,* too. Figure out how to get a columnist to be interested in you, then take a crack at it. Or reverse the process by using a search engine like Google to find articles about bands you sound like, find the name of the writer who wrote the piece, the name of the publication they wrote it for, and then hunt them down. You can also research specific writers this way to gauge their taste and determine if you're the type of band they'll be inclined to champion.

You might be surprised by the responses you get. Your story, if pitched correctly, might sound really fresh and alive to someone else. Editors love national stories, for instance, especially stories about trends, and if you can prove to an editor or writer that the trend you're involved in is going on in Denver, Salt Lake City, and San Francisco, they might jump on it. "There are many, many opportunities," says Aleba Gartner. "Papers are full of sections, writers, reporters, soft news, hard news, and gossip. It's all there to be taken advantage of. It takes extra time, but if you focus on one thing, you might get it and that could be a gold nugget."

Even though you may have done a lot of research to determine a writer's taste, don't hesitate to send someone something that might not seem like a perfect fit. Take a chance. Writers don't only want to write about the same type of music all the time. Let them decide if they like it. If you're a folk musician with a really focused album and great lyrics, who's to say someone who writes about punk music isn't going to fall in love with your material? Good music is good music, and serious music writers will filter through the crap to get to your stuff if you make it available. Whenever you take chances, you open yourself up to possibilities that wouldn't have existed if you followed the rules.

Once you've developed a sizable list of editorial contacts, save the names, numbers, e-mail addresses, and regular mail addresses in a new database, then begin contacting the most likely candidates by phone or e-mail to ask if they'd be willing to consider your record or upcoming gig for review. That's right—it's cold-calling time, and it's probably going to feel uncomfortable the first few times you do it, but it's your career, and if you're not going to do the grunt work nobody is going to do it in your place unless you pay them.

Once you get a writer on the phone, let them know if you've been reading their articles. Don't lie about it; they'll figure it out, trust me. Do your homework. Mention something they wrote, then compliment them for their exquisite taste or clever insights. Then tell them that you'll be sending them a package with music you think they're really going to like as soon as you hang up the phone, let them know it'll be there in a few days, then thank them for their time.

Do this as many times as you can tolerate in a short span, then put together each press kit (minus the soon-to-come press clipping) in a padded envelope, making sure the envelopes are large enough so that you don't have to cram the materials inside. Address the envelopes legibly, then write a personalized note to each specific editor reminding them of your recent phone call or e-mail—make absolutely sure you spell their name correctly. In the note, review what you talked about, suggest a review of the record you've included in the kit, then tell them you'd appreciate hearing their feedback when they get a chance.

Don't stop there. Make sure to invite them to an upcoming show, and offer to comp their admission at the door by putting them on the guest list if they show up. Even offer to buy them a drink if they've got the time. Make them feel like you'd be honored by their presence, and do whatever you have to do to get them interested. If all that fails, compare yourself to something you know they already like (but make sure the comparison is viable).

If writing a friendly note isn't your style, try composing a short fact sheet with bullets, says Gartner. "Tell them, 'I'm performing at Merkin Hall in three weeks, and I hope you or one of your colleagues can attend the performance for review,' then direct them to your Website for more info on your band and color images to download in case they have room to run a photo, even if there isn't room for review or preview."

Once you've written some type of personal acknowledgment, double-check that you're putting it in the envelope with the right address, staple it shut (sealing it is unnecessary and only annoys editors when the padding rips open and covers their clothing with it fibrous mist), then drop them in the mail or, better yet, walk them over to each respective editor's office and tell the receptionist you need to hand the editor the package personally. In the worst case, he or she will tell you to leave the package, and in the best case you might actually meet the editor in person and help your cause that much more.

Just keep in mind that contacting editors and writers in the hope of getting coverage shouldn't be a one-sided affair. Your interaction with them should be mutually beneficial. They're not dummies—they know what you want, so you have to let them know you understand their needs. Make their jobs and their decisions about you easier by explaining why your band is such a great story.

"It's very important to emphasize anything that makes you stand apart from the other groups within your same genre," says Gartner. "By that, I mean if you do anything that is a first, a premiere, the most unusual—that's the story, that's the news. The press isn't interested in writing yet another profile. They're always looking for the challenge within the story, something that made the artist overcome something."

Don't be bashful about making a follow-up call or writing a short e-mail to the writers you contacted to see if they were planning on covering you in some way. Give them a week or two, but no longer, and if you still haven't heard from them, reach out to them again. When you contact them, ask if they gave your record any consideration. If they did, they'll let you know, and if they forgot about it, your call will remind them to check it out. Really, don't worry about making the follow-up calls. It lets people know you're serious about your music, and they'll respect you more for treating it professionally.

Making follow-up calls is probably the single most important activity you can undertake when it comes to self-promotion, and it's also the one thing that most musicians consistently fail to do. Think about it: Your career is at stake. Is it worth it for you to trust that people will do what they say they'll do, or is it better for you to make sure that they do it? You don't have to be a nag. When you talk to people for the first time about your band, let them know you'll be sending them a CD package, and at the same time tell them you'll call them back in a week to see what they think about it. It sends the message that you're serious, it shows that you're concerned, and it lets them know that you are willing to work hard to get what you want.

They won't think you're weak if you call them back—they may not have time for you that moment, but it's totally acceptable and expected. In fact, if you don't make follow-up phone calls, you might be dismissed as someone who didn't care enough and didn't deserve anything to begin with. Nothing good comes easily. You've got to put the legwork in and keep people you need in your corner focused on what you think is important.

You don't need to be pushy, just be courteous and professional. Respect the fact that they have deadlines and lots of different responsibilities. These are human beings with real job pressures and very distinct tastes. Once you've taken the time to read their articles, you'll learn about their opinions and understand some of their needs. If you empower yourself with this knowledge and try to keep things in perspective, it will only help your cause.

Yes, I know this sounds like a lot of hustling for a measly press clipping, but it's worth it. You're not going to be rewarded right out of the gate with front-page coverage, but once you start getting covered it'll help build momentum. That'll show in your press kit and beyond, but it's going to take time. Attracting attention and respect from the press is a gradual, cumulative process. You can't expect a response after the very first introduction or e-mail if you're contacting someone who doesn't know you, hasn't seen you perform, or hasn't heard your music. This process is about planting seeds. Get them to listen, get them to see you, then help them make up their own minds.

Do not forget to thank the writer for what they said (unless it was completely negative, which does happen from time to time), and from then on make a point of inviting them to future shows. You want them on your side from here on out. If they liked you enough to write about you in the first place, they'll probably follow you as you progress through your career and will champion your cause as long as you keep them in the loop. They should become one of your first and most reliable points of contact from here on out.

Physically Copy Those Clippings

Once you receive a press clipping, photocopy it or scan it at the highest possible resolution so that you can reproduce it en masse. If the clipping takes up more than one page or is broken up into columns or short bits, isolate the entire article—combining sections from separate pages if need be—so that the reader won't be distracted by other stories on the page. No matter what, you want the source publication's name and logo, as well as the date of the publication to appear clearly on the top of the clipping, followed by whatever text and photos were used to praise your greatness. Do this on each successive page of the clipping.

If you have to do this on hardcopy text (the actual newspaper or magazine as opposed to an article available on line), do it very carefully with an Exacto knife or scissors, and use clear art glue to attach each portion of the clipping to a white piece of paper; try to get the edges glued down tightly so that lines don't show up when you reproduce your master document. Once you've got the entire clipping on a sheet of paper, make a copy of it. You may need to use some sort of white-out product to remove unwanted lines and artifacts that appear around the edges of the various pieces and sections of articles on your master copy, but you'll eventually get it to the point where it looks as if it was originally one continuous piece. Make sure everything is centered and level, adjust the contrast so that the text isn't either too light or dark, then start making copies for your press kits.

Your copies should be reproduced with the intention of matching the quality of original source, but color reproduction isn't necessary unless the clipping itself comes from a highly regarded publication or the picture or illustration that you're copying demands it. Basically, if you're sending a clip to someone who truly needs to be impressed, do it in color, otherwise don't waste the money.

Once You Have a Press Clipping
You should always try to get press coverage for yourself—it should be a non-stop activity—but getting that first press clipping is a notable achievement because so many things can follow. For starters, you'll definitely be able to use it in your press kit, proving that someone else thought you were worthy of media coverage. What you're going for is the domino-effect: One review begets others, and soon enough you'll be able to select articles and reviews from a pile to tell your story for you, even if the person who will leaf through them only reads the headlines and sources.

There's no need to put a copy of every article that's ever been written about you in your press kit. Just choose the ones from prominent sources or those that offer glowing praise. Packing every single clipping in there might have some impact in terms of the overall weight (literally and figuratively) your press kit will have, but it's more expensive for you to reproduce and ship the kits, and a little too much reading to expect from people who don't have the time or inclination to read through eight different articles about you after listening to your demo and reading your bio.

ONCE THE PRESS KIT IS COMPLETE
When you've finally got your press kit components assembled, they should have a clean and organized look. You don't need to create some sort of branded folder to hold all the items unless you're flush with money. The envelope you send them in will be sufficient. If you took this process seriously, the quality and care you showed in putting together all of the individual components will be obvious, and that will say something to the person who receives it.

"I can't tell you how many press kits I've seen from indie PR firms who get paid a lot of money that contain crumpled, crappy bios, and unreadable photocopies," says Karen Wiessen. "If it's tattered or I simply can't read it, it's going in the garbage. I don't have time, and neither does anyone else. Knowing how many packages people at clubs and in A&R receive, why would you bother? If you're a brand new act and the person opening your package has never heard of you and knows nothing about you, there's a crappy Xerox in there, the kit is in disarray, who has the time for that? We live in a very time-sensitive world, so your kit has got to be eye-catching, mind-catching, professional, and must look like you cared enough to make something interesting happen."

Decide how many kits you want to send out, and then go buy enough padded envelopes and mailing labels to accommodate them. Don't get cheap with the envelopes. Regular mail is rough on CD jewel boxes, and you don't want yours to arrive cracked or scratched. Spend the extra money on the padded envelopes—they'll protect your goods, and you'll be able to write them off as a business expense.

Now start thinking long and hard about the types of people you want to interest with your music (and why). When you know what you're trying to accomplish by sending the kits out, refer to your contact list or database and target those specific people who need to know more about your band. Their full contact information should end up on a separate spreadsheet or list.

This new spreadsheet should include booking agents at local clubs, radio station program directors, band managers, tour promoters, festival/conference committees, and anyone else who might be interested in latching on to what you're doing. Make sure to leave room for notes next to each contact's name so that you will know who you sent a kit to, when you sent it, when you plan to make a follow-up call or e-mail, and what the ultimate result or response was. And don't forget to ask people in your existing network to provide you with new contacts who might be interested in your music. Name dropping will open doors for you that might otherwise never get opened.

If you've exhausted all your current contacts and still feel that you need more coverage, there are numerous Websites and industry reference books that list personnel at record labels, publishing companies, radio stations, entertainment-law offices, booking agents, etc. But don't just send them out without first trying to reach out to people. You'll be much more likely to meet with success if you've already established a relationship with the person on the receiving end. Do your research, figure out who can help you in the area you want to succeed in, and get those press kits out there.

On line, CD-ROM, and print resources for industry contact information include the following:

Reference Books and CD-ROMs
The Indie Bible (www.indiebible.com)

Billboard International Buyer's Guide (www.billboard.com)
The Musician's Atlas (www.musiciansatlas.com)
Bacon's Media Directories (www.bacons.com)
The Music Business Registry (www.musicregistry.com)
The Galaris Musicians Directory (www.galaris.com/GMD.html)
Recording Industry Sourcebook (www.isourcebook.com)

Online References

http://directory.google.com/Top/Business/Arts_and_Entertainment/Music/

   Directories/
www.musicalamerica.com
www.HitQuarters.com/
www.themusicindex.com/index.htm
www.sonicswitchblade.com
www.showcase-music.com
www.go2audio.com/
www.taxi.com
www.iuma.com
www.garageband.com

www.musicisland.com/
www.buzzsonic.tv
www.musicphonebook.com
www.showbizcontacts.com
www.RSDEntertainment.com
www.a2gmusic.com
www.ampcast.com
www.artistpro.com
www.aandronline.com
www.recordlabelresource.com

The most cost-effective way to mail out a press kit is via regular U.S. mail. Don't bother with expensive overnight carriers unless it's got to get there no matter what on a particular day. In any case, make sure to prominently write the name of your band and/or a band member's name the recipient will recognize on the outside of the package. The person at the receiving end should be able to find your unopened package on their desk without much searching.

YOU ARE YOUR PRESS KIT

There will be numerous occasions over the next few years when you'll be confronted with opportunities to pitch your band to someone who can make a difference, and when those opportunities come up, you've got to be your own press kit. It can happen at a party, out on the street, in a club or restaurant, or while you're leafing through the in-flight magazine on a plane. Out of nowhere you find yourself face-to-face with someone who can help your band's cause. What are you going to say?

People in the business world call it the thirty-second elevator conversation, and they constantly stress the importance of being well prepared for those chance meetings with influential people. It's important to be able to speak eloquently and succinctly about your band to anyone you might meet, but it's especially important to be able to make a great impression on someone in the business.

Your ability to condense and package your message is key. You've got to be creative in order to capture and keep their attention, but you've also got to be sincere and substantial enough to maximize the small window of time you're granted. I'm not talking about simply saying something coherent about your band. I'm talking about confidently launching into a heartfelt pitch that emotionally engages the person you're speaking to and sticks with them when the conversation is over. You want to walk away knowing that you initiated a conversation that they'll want to continue.

That's not going to be the feeling you have if you don't prepare yourself by coming up with talking points ahead of time and practicing them until it feels comfortable and natural for you to say it all. Trust me, this is not something you should feel comfortable doing spontaneously. Some people are natural-born salesmen, but chances are you're not—you'd know it if you were, and you wouldn't be reading this book. You need to craft a message, rehearse how you'll say it, and deliver it fluidly so that it comes out polished while still sounding spontaneous.

The thirty-second elevator conversation isn't just about you talking and sealing the record deal. You're not in a vacuum, you're in a conversation. While it's your responsibility to initiate it, you've got to deliver your message while fielding questions and looking to see if the person you're talking to seems interested. The only way you'll be able to listen and respond without losing your train of thought is to have your end of the conversation down cold. Know it like the back of your hand.

Before you start trying to craft a statement, get yourself ready by thinking about the issues listed below and writing down your thoughts:

1. Describe your band and it's brand. If you read the earlier chapter on branding, you've already done the legwork here. Identify what makes your band relevant and figure out how to sell that idea without proselytizing.

2. What kind of help are you looking for? Once you've told someone what you do, you've got to follow up by telling them how they can help you. How will their assistance change the course of what you're doing?

3. What's the benefit to someone else helping you? Why should someone invest their time and energy? What's in it for them?

Once you've got these ideas in mind, condense it all into a compelling monologue and read it aloud while you time yourself to see how long it takes. You don't have to nail it to thirty seconds, but it shouldn't be too much longer than that. Edit it for length if necessary and keep timing it until it's in the right range. You're going for short and sweet, remember?

If the language feels right and the length of the pitch is within reason, practice saying it to a few different people and see what their impressions are. You've got to read it like you'd say it, though—a monotonous drone won't do. When you're done, ask for comments and make adjustments accordingly. You could even record yourself to hear how you sound. Just be honest about your performance. Once you're comfortable with the ins and outs of your presentation, try it out for real on anyone you meet. Trust me, you'll know when it's working, and you'll see it in their eyes and body language if it isn't.

By doing all this legwork in advance, you'll be ready to pounce when opportunity comes knocking. When it does happen, chances are you'll have some idea what the person's interests are before you start with your spiel, so try to cater your message to match their interests. You're looking for natural segues to steer the conversation where you want it to go, and if you can make it seem as though you're just casually talking about yourself rather than running through a prepared speech, you'll be able to capture their attention. Just keep things brief, and try not to overload them with information.

Make sure you finish your pitch by asking for whatever type of help or assistance you're looking for. If you don't ask, you won't get it. If that question feels too straightforward, ask if they'd be willing to continue your conversation another time over lunch, a drink, phone, or e-mail. Let them know you can send them a full press kit if they'd like. It may feel a little awkward to do this, but you've got to strike while the iron is hot. If they say "no" for some reason, thank them for their time and hand them your card with the hope that they'll pass it on to someone they know who might be interested in you when that time comes.

You're not a telemarketer, so don't impersonate one. Have fun with this. Your ultimate goal is to create interest and command respect, so treat it as a heartfelt conversation and be passionate. And don't assume that everyone's interested just because they appear to be listening—look at their eyes and facial expressions, and be sensitive to these signs. There's no need to race through your entire pitch if you've already sold someone on your band. If you pay attention to how people respond, you'll learn to tell the difference between "yeah" and "eh," and if you're prepared to sell yourself to anyone at anytime, your chance will come.

chapter seven

CREATING AN EFFECTIVE WEBSITE

I f you stood up on your chair ten years ago and declared the Internet was going to turn the music industry upside down, people probably would've said you were high on crack. Major corporations traditionally had the money, power, and cachet to sign and break new talent, they had the means and the clout needed to promote and market established talent to the masses, they controlled the retail distribution network, they influenced the music press with endless junkets, they stuffed the record bins with what they thought would sell, and they worked hand-in-hand with commercial radio to saturate the airwaves with their products. The very thought that some upstarts touting an over-hyped geek-technology would change all that seemed ludicrous.

THE INTERNET TAKES OVER

But a few years later, major-label CEOs recognized that the Internet was more than just a passing trend and no longer discounted it as a competitive force. The Internet got up in the major labels' faces so quickly that they're wasn't a chance to develop a strategy to control or contain it. Soon the Internet not only posed a threat to the record industry's way of doing business, it placed its very survival in question.

File-sharing peer-to-peer Websites like Napster took a vicious bite out of the major labels' collective behind, by enabling consumers to download what they wanted for free rather than buying it. Recognizing that their lunch was being eaten, the labels responded with threats and lawsuits— they couldn't stop what was going on and couldn't move quickly enough to capitalize on it themselves. Consumer demand drove the labels to the brink, and they found themselves barely able to hold back the floodwaters as the tide continued to rise.

And rise it did. Peer-to-peer services plagued the major labels and drew attention to the fact that CDs were—and still are—overpriced. Online retailers sprouted up like mushrooms, forcing every brick-and-mortar record retail chain still in business to adjust its model to sell music on line.

Commercial radio's disdain for diversity and its computerized music programming drove an increasing number of people to customized online radio stations, time-shifted programming, podcasts, and archival streamed audio feeds for their entertainment. Today, with commercial-free satellite radio poised to reach critical mass in the next few years, it's only a matter of time before impersonal terrestrial radio formats go the way of the dinosaur, and not a second too soon.

The major labels tried to buy and absorb what they couldn't control as a way to stave off their own extinction and to some degree they saved themselves in the act, but the Internet has inarguably changed the record business. Major label consolidation may have been a painful experience for those involved, but in the end it will prove to have benefitted musicians, music fans, and music in general.

The Internet forced all of these issues, and as a result, artists have realized that "making it" is no longer an all-or-nothing proposition, solely dependent on approval and support from the music industry giants. Thanks to search engines, e-mail lists, bulletin boards, band portals, shared links with other band Websites, mp3 downloads, podcasts, and e-commerce, independent bands can use the Internet to do it all. You can research and establish contacts, book gigs, draw crowds, sell records, plan tours, and create interest from the media without the help of a major label. Above all, you can use the Internet to drive traffic to your Website, which, if used correctly, can be a powerful marketing tool for your music career.

WHY DO YOU WANT A WEBSITE?

As far as band Websites are concerned, there's no guarantee anyone will stop by just because you hang a shingle out on the superhighway. Building a strong online presence doesn't just happen because you think it's your right or your destiny. You're going to need a plan if you expect people to show up, stick around, and come back for more.

"The Internet isn't the point—it's just an in-between," says Derek Sivers, founder and president of the independent band e-commerce site CD Baby. And he's right—a Website is just a tool for communicating. What are you trying to communicate? Before you dive into the creation of your band Website, ask yourself what goal you are trying to achieve. Every other band may have one, but "me too" isn't a good enough reason. You hopefully have greater aspirations than simply doing what everyone else is doing.

What is a Website going to do to help you achieve success? Do you think it'll help your music receive greater notoriety? Will it help you increase your fan base by reaching an audience outside your geographical region? Will it somehow attract attention from record labels and the media? Or is it just a novel way to let people discover who you are, listen to your music, buy your CDs, and get on your mailing list (hey, good idea)? If you answered "yes" to any or all of the above, that's great, because they're all valid reasons. You just need to keep that goal in focus as you get deeper into the process.

Regardless of your ultimate goal, your band Website should function as a flytrap. People are out there looking everywhere for musical sustenance, so your site has got to be appealing enough to attract their attention and sticky enough to make them stay put. Your music is the bait. That's what's going to help you attract new fans, keep the ones you've already got, and influence their decision to buy your CDs and attend your gigs. When you can do that successfully, the media will start paying attention, and when the media notices, the record labels will soil their own trousers to find out what all the fuss is about.

TWO OPTIONS

Getting your Website up and running is going to take a lot of work, so think carefully about how much time and money you can afford to put into it upfront. If you're smitten with the DIY spirit you can certainly build your Website yourself, but you really should think about whether the time you'll spend figuring out how to do it is worth the amount of money you'll save paying a professional to do it on your behalf. But even if you'd rather put your Website's creation in the hands of a pro, you're still going to play a major role in the conception and design of the site. It's a long process even if you're not doing the heavy lifting. That means coming up with solid, executable ideas; creating the content (audio files, text, graphics, and interactivity); registering a domain name and finding a host service (an Internet service provider, a.k.a. ISP) that's capable of meeting your needs and your monthly budget; and putting it all together, making it work, testing it, launching it, maintaining it, and updating it on a semi-regular basis.

Whichever path you choose, keep in mind, it might not be necessary to go full bore right out of the gate. It's often easier to meet the minimum requirements first and build out from there when the time is right. The conservative approach may not feel sexy, but it's smart.

Do It Yourself

I'm not going to launch into a long discussion on the mechanics of building a Website—that would be a book unto itself. When you're ready to address the specifics on your own site, you should refer to books like David Nevue's *How to Successfully Promote Your Music on the Internet (www.musicbizacademy.com/ bookstore/htpromotemusic.htm),* or how-to books about building Websites, such as Elizabeth Castro's *HTML 4 for the World Wide Web: VQS.*

There are many relatively inexpensive software tools available to build a basic site. Microsoft's FrontPage (idiot proof) and MacroMedia's Dreamweaver (used by professional designers) are the two leading applications for DIYers. They both come pre-packaged with numerous templates that any moderately computer literate person can use to build a Website without any programming required. Just plug in your info and you're done.

If you're looking to sell merchandise on your site, you'll need to do some additional work. More elaborate sites with online retailing require software that connects to financial institutions so that you can process credit-card transactions. If you're interested, check out the open source ecommerce application called Oscommerce *(www.oscommerce.com).*

Let a Pro Handle It

Unless you, a bandmate, or a very close, very kind friend is a gifted artist, designer, writer, and architect you'll likely want to hire someone who can create the site to your specifications. There are plenty of designers out there, but you've got to know what you want before you go shopping around to find the right person to build your site. With your specs in hand, you'll be able to get cost estimates from potential candidates while weeding out the wannabes who can't do what you're going to need.

What are your specs? Well, that depends on your overall vision, but there are some basic points that you'll definitely want to keep in mind. You know you're going to require audio files, a bio, a way for users to sign-up for e-mail updates, and an area to display current band news and photos. You want intuitive navigation, quick load times for every page (even for low-bandwidth losers), a flexible design that accounts for various monitor sizes (640 x 480 pixels should be the smallest), programming code that works in all conventional browsers, and minimal reliance on software plug-ins (none if possible).

Finding the Right Match

If you present this basic list to any designer worth their salt along with an approximate budget estimate, the good ones will be able to come up with a proposal that meets your needs and your budget. Seriously, the world is loaded with Web designers, so finding one should be easy. Of course, finding the *right* one will take some doing. To start your search, post an ad on a site like *www.craigslist.com* or in a local newspaper, or just let your friends know you need references for good Web designers. You'll probably get more responses than you need. (Hiring a design firm enables you to speed up the process considerably and usually guarantees a high level of professionalism, but such firms will typically charge twice what an independent designer will charge.

You're looking for someone with prior experience building sites, a verifiable portfolio you can refer to, and references you can check. Any candidate who meets all three requirements is worth talking to. Let them know your specifications, your budget limitations, and your expectations, then ask them to put together a proposal that defines their process and sets forth a timeline to have your site designed, built, and active.

You can expect a little back and forth as you narrow down the field of potential candidates, but the right person will come into focus quickly as you start negotiating with the final candidates. Ultimately you've got to go with your gut, but in my opinion it's better to err on the side of caution. Choose someone whose strength lies in building Websites rather than taking a chance on someone who's got a flair for design but less of a track record with the nuts and bolts.

What It Will Cost You

Fees for building band Websites are usually project-based rather than hourly, and designers will likely try to work with whatever budget you've got unless it's totally unrealistic for the type and amount of work you want done. "My price varies depending on the project," says Bill Curran, a Boston-based freelance Web designer *(www.evillittleclown.com)* who designs artist Websites for independent bands, as well as signed acts on Sony and Roadrunner Records. "I try to keep my price range as rubbery, fluid, and open as possible. Some kids don't have the bucks, so I try to help. I ask them what they think it's worth. They'll throw out a price, and I'll be honest with them. I get them to pick what they're looking to spend, and then I can work around that."

Your budget will dictate the level of designer you work with and/or what type of Website you can ultimately build. Chances are you'll find yourself in the position of wanting more than your budget allows, but that doesn't mean you can't get what you want if you're willing to take some chances. "My entry-level fee for a very minimal Website that doesn't use Flash and only provides the architecture to showcase information the band already has about themselves is roughly $2,000," says Marshall Jones, a New York-based freelance Web designer, "but there are a lot of younger designers out there who will only charge $500 for the same thing."

For students or designers who need to build their portfolio, building your site is a great opportunity even if they barely break even to do the work, says Jones. "Students and designers fresh out of school are a good resource for bands with no money because they need the work on their résumé and the dough in their pocket, but even designers like me are often willing to tone down what they charge to meet your budget."

Many people assume it's worthwhile to haggle with Web designers for the lowest possible price, but if you push it too far your Website will likely suffer as a result. "Cheap doesn't mean good," explains Curran. "When you go into a studio, that costs money. You can do a day in a really great studio or week in a terrible one. Which one do you want? It's the same type of thing with Web design. You're paying the person to build something that represents you. If there are five guys in a band, if you pool together your money, it's not that much coming from five guys. A good site is a smart investment."

Working With Your Designer
Once you've settled on your designer, meet with them to nail down exactly what the site will be. Discuss your specifications once again and talk about the timeline for making the site come together. Keep in mind that your site must be in keeping with your music and your brand—that's what you're promoting, and that's what your Website must serve—not the Web designer's idea of what would bolster their portfolio. Colors, graphics, typefaces, and the overall layout should work in tandem to drive home your brand message.

Develop a strategy to achieve something cool together. You will be responsible for delivering the content to them—audio, text, and photos— and they will take care of everything else from there until there's something coherent to look at. "Everything else" means making sure the content looks appealing, the pages load quickly, the functionality is consistent, and the navigation is intuitive on every page. Remember: Less is more, and it's also much easier to manage. Once you've determined what it's going to take to build your site in time and money, get busy.

DOMAIN NAMES AND HOSTING
Before you start creating content, you've got some leg work to take care of. You've got to pick out an appropriately catchy (and available) domain name for your site, and you also need to pick a service provider to host it.

Name That Site
A domain name is what is technically known as a Universal Resource Locator (more commonly known as your URL), which serves as the unique identifier to guide people to your Website's address on line (ex: *www.yourbandssite.com* or *www.totallyuniquebanddomainname4u.com*). It's

not a law, but your domain absolutely must have your band's name in it and should be memorable or obvious. Potential visitors should be able to find it—and remember it—without much thought.

When you've come up with a list of potential domain names, check to see if your favorite domain is available by visiting any of the online domain registrars. The two primary providers of domain names are *www.register.com* and *www.networksolutions.com,* but you can find cheaper ones that offer the same service by typing "domain registration" into a search engine.

If your prospective domain is already in use by someone else, subtly adapt it by adding a hyphenated word to it such as "-music" or "-band." If that doesn't work, consider an alternative name or check to see if other domain suffixes are available with the same basic domain name. (Domain suffixes designate categories of Websites by type, with ".com" being the most common. Both ".net," or ".org" are acceptable alternatives, but ".com" is the most popular.) Whatever you do, don't set up your domain on someone else's site—it might be cost-effective, but all that says is you're not serious enough to have your own domain. That's not the impression you want to project.

Find a Host

Once you've settled on a domain name and registered it, you've got to find a host provider. (Hosts provide space on their servers where your Website exists.) Your designer can probably suggest a couple hosts to choose from, and you'll definitely want their input when you're shopping around, because the one you select needs to meet certain technical criteria to accommodate your needs.

Basically, your host service needs to offer adequate disc space (at least 500MB to 1,000MB), Web statistics, platform support, and ample bandwidth to enable multiple simultaneous visitors. Disc space is essentially how much file space you'll have on their server, which is important if you intend to offer lots of mp3s and high-resolution photos. Web statistics will tell you things like how many visitors come to your site, how long they're staying, and what other sites are linked to yours. Platform support becomes an issue if you're considering forums, bulletin boards, or chatrooms that require a specific programming format. Bandwidth restrictions probably won't be much of an issue, at least not at first, unless you are reasonably certain that you'll have a lot of simultaneous users downloading files.

Your designer will (or at least should) know what your needs are in this regard. Let them know who your host service is, and they should be able to take it from there. If you find yourself on the fence when choosing between different levels of service, think hard about what components you really need on your site and try to gauge whether your ambitions are cost-effective in the short term and flexible enough for expansion in the long term.

Once you and your designer have selected a host, put up a simple placeholder to let people know a site is being built. Once you've taken care of this, you can start creating your content in earnest.

STAY IN CONTROL

One last thing: Make sure before your site has been uploaded that you are the legal owner and possessor of its source code, its URL, and its database. You need be able to update the site whenever you want, and you don't want to be held hostage by someone if there's ever a disagreement down the line. It's your Website. You paid for it. Make sure you own it and that the site is, in fact, registered in your name. You can check Website ownership by searching the Whois database at *Netsol.com*.

MAKE YOUR SITE USER FRIENDLY

Before I move on to discuss the content components you'll need on your site, let's get something straight. Time and attention spans are short and as a rule you've got one shot to capture someone's interest. You're building this Website to attract attention to your music from potential fans and industry types. The last thing you want to do is to piss those same people off because they can't navigate through it easily or because it takes too long to load. Above all, make the site user friendly.

Ditch the Bells and Whistles

For starters, there is absolutely no good reason for using Flash, Shockwave, or any other plug-in. Many Web designers will disagree with that statement, but they're only seeing things from a design perspective and not from the user's viewpoint. The use of plug-ins creates a barrier to entry for anyone who doesn't have the plug-in installed on their computer when they arrive at your Website—the likelihood of them downloading it, installing it, and returning to your Website is close to zero, and even if they did, what other than your music could possibly make it worth all that?

Be realistic. You're not going to change labor-intensive animation sequences on a daily or weekly basis, so they're going to get painfully old for repeat visitors. Outrageous graphics and gratuitous interactions shouldn't be the catalyst for your site. The focus is supposed to be on the music and the band. Animation is fluff and has nothing to do with your music. Don't spend the time, money, or effort.

Similarly, if you don't use plug-ins then there's no need for ridiculous "loading" animations before your main page appears. Loading animations are those small, annoying graphics that appear onscreen as placeholders to entertain you while the stuff you really want loads in the background. These animations are the equivalent of commercials before the previews at a movie theater—no one wants to see them. Same goes for the "enter here" buttons on splash pages. Both are unnecessary steps. Make your content simple enough that it doesn't need any significant pre-load time. Bring the user right to the main page so that they can decide where they want to go next. Doing it any other way prevents the user from getting to the content they came in search of.

Navigation

If you want people to come back to your site after their first visit, make sure it's easy for them to figure out how to move around between the various pages. All of a user's possible options should be obvious the moment they land on the main page, and once they start looking around they should be able to maneuver around your site effortlessly.

Tell people what content exists and make it quick and hassle-free for them to get to it. Easy-to-read buttons with obvious names like "bio," "buy music," "discography," and "photos" will help immensely. Remember, function over form. Keep the processes transparent and obvious; save the aura and mystique for your music.

Your main page should be the first page users see when they arrive at your site, and it should serve as a table of contents to show them what is available on the site. Don't just assume that it makes sense. Check it yourself and let other people take it for a spin to confirm it. The navigation on the main page and each successive layer of content on successive pages should work without creating extra steps to get from here to there. If it doesn't, create a site map layout that shows all the possible avenues between the various content pages. That should serve as a map to crosscheck the navigation on your site.

SITE CONTENT

Now that we've gotten that squared away, it's time to focus on content. First of all, remember how I bored you to death with all that talk about branding back in Chapter 5, Branding You? Your Website must announce your brand on every page, whether it's through the use of your logo, photos, or the way you tell your story throughout the site. Visitors should always know they're on your Website, and your designer will achieve this through the strategic application of photos, images, graphics, and text that reinforces your brand concept. Visit any major-label Website and look at their artist sites and you'll see what I mean: Each band's name and/or logo appears on every page, there's a consistent aesthetic throughout every page on the site, and the language and photos are in keeping with brand.

So with your brand in mind as you begin, your site should consist of the following components: Audio files, a bio, a news section, an e-mail sign-up list, a photo section, and an e-commerce section (or a link to an e-commerce site) for your CDs and associated merchandise.

And don't forget to put your contact info on every single page. This is very important. It doesn't have to be the focal point on every page, but it should be obviously located in the same spot on every page. You want to give visitors every opportunity to reach out to you.

Audio Files

Your Website exists to promote your product, so don't think for a minute that you've got to be reserved about promoting it. That's the whole point. Push your music into the limelight—don't be bashful.

In most cases people will visit your site to check out your music, so it's imperative that you make it abundant and easy to find, like low-hanging fruit. This doesn't mean you should make every song you've ever recorded available, but you should provide enough music for people to really get a sense of your songwriting ability, your musicianship, your sound, and your stylistic range. They should be able to listen to music on your site and know right away whether they want to buy one of your CDs or attend one of your shows.

Don't get precious or paranoid about giving your songs away—that's penny-wise, dollar-stupid. It's far better to have lots of people downloading your free music than nobody paying attention because you're only offering thirty seconds of each song. After all, it's not like you're giving your entire catalogue away. If they like the sound of what they're hearing for free they'll drop money to own the real thing. Besides, you're not going to convert your audio files at an audiophile-accepted bit rate, so they're not going to sound as good as your finished product—unless, of course, your album doesn't sound good to begin with.

The sound quality of your audio files must be good enough for users to get a sense of what your music really sounds like. There's an appreciable difference between acceptable and respectable—you don't catch flies with vinegar, you catch them with honey. Make your audio files sound sweet.

Offer mp3 downloads and streaming audio files so that users can choose how they want to listen to your music, but make sure you optimize your audio files for playback on the Web regardless of the audio format you make available. Optimization essentially means encoding the files so that they sound their best when downloaded from an online source. Most music is initially mastered for playback through a stereo, not a computer, but if it was done properly the levels will be as hot as possible, meaning that you won't have to struggle too much to convert them for use on line.

Optimization isn't brain surgery, but it's a process that requires an understanding of basic audio mastering techniques like normalization, equalization, and compression to make sure that the volume is consistent, the frequencies are sonorous, and dynamic range sounds normal without any sudden peaks or dropouts. For an introduction to optimization techniques, check out Josh Beggs' article at *http://Web .oreilly.com/news/Web audio_1200.html* or refer to any of the tutorials regularly found in recording magazines.

If you're a glutton for punishment or just simply curious, you might consider adding some type of polling or voting functionality to your site. This would theoretically give visitors an opportunity to give you feedback about your music. I say "theoretically" because you never know what some people are going to say. Constructive criticism or high praise is always welcome, but there's no way to control how people will vote and no way to really take direction from it. On the other hand, it does make people feel a part of the experience, which may in and of itself be worth the effort. Check out *www.misterpoll.com, www.pollit.com, www.antibs.com,* or any of the multiple free or fee-based polling tools available on line.

About the Band
There's no reason to create a new bio and photos for your Website if you've already put together a press kit. In fact, you should probably edit your current bio to make it shorter for use on line. Why? I'm hoping to protect you from your narcissistic self.

Technically speaking you could make your online bio as long as you like, but people seem to have even less of an attention span when reading information on Websites. Try to keep your bio concise enough so that people can read it in its entirety without having to scroll down the screen or jump to additional pages. If you really feel the need to tell your story at greater length, let other people do it for you. Provide links to all your press clippings.

News and Events
If people decide that they like your music they're going to want to know what you're up to, so it's probably a good idea to post some type of news or upcoming events section. Design a text window that's relatively easy to update, but don't use any of that cheesy perpetually crawling text or corny

animations. Your Website isn't a stock ticker in Times Square. Make it easy for people to read—they shouldn't have to strain their eyes or move their head to decipher it—and provide all the key information in headline form (what's happening, when, and where) so that they can decide if they want to read more right away.

This is the place to include information on upcoming shows. People *do* want to know when your next gig is. I can't tell you how many times I've heard people say, "Hey, if I knew you were playing I would have come." Make sure there's an area that lists upcoming shows or complete tour dates, and don't forget to include all the crucial information about each gig so that people can leave your Website knowing everything they need to actually come see you perform.

Make it easy for your fans to find this information and give them the additional opportunity to sign up for e-mail updates about upcoming shows so that they won't even have to log onto your site to find out about your shows.

Images

Let's face it, audio files and information on the band are all well and good, but you'll need to throw in some photos, too. Not only does it liven up your site from a design perspective and reinforce your brand image (that damn brand thing again), but it also sates the rabid visual curiosity of fans and music-industry types alike.

Create a page where people can go to look at whatever band photos you have available, but don't force them to wait while every photo you have loads. Instead, have a main photo and thumbnail images of the photos that people can click on if they're interested. High-resolution images are great if you have them, and they'll come in handy once you start getting covered in newspapers and magazines—art directors will be happy to check out all your photos and choose the ones they want to use for reproduction in their publication.

E-mail Lists

Building an online e-mail list is the first step toward creating an actual community of fans. Users should be able to enter their e-mail address knowing that you won't sell your e-mail list to someone who'll spam them into living hell. Their privacy must be respected—make sure you let them know their information will not be shared or sold to anyone.

Don't just assume that every name and address on your e-mail list is real. Instead, set up your mailing list so that it sends a confirmation e-mail that requires the person to respond before they're added to your list. This ensures that you're sending e-mails to real e-mail addresses of people who want to receive your information. Check out *www.thesitewizard.com/reviews/ yhoogroups.shtml* for information on using third-party mailing list services to handle the messy aspects of sending out your info if you're not up to the task yourself.

If you want to get really serious about marketing yourself you can ask people who sign up for your e-mails to submit more detailed information about themselves, but unless you've really got a plan for using that information and are willing to offer people an incentive to fill out some massive demographic questionnaire, save it for later. Right now you're trying to acquire more fans, not scare them away.

Selling Your Merchandise

Any product you try to sell at your shows should be available for sale on line. That means CDs as well as any other band-related merchandise you have, whether it's T-shirts, bobblehead dolls, or drink coasters. This can be done from your site or you can have a third-party company do it for you, but you should understand the clear advantages that each choice offers.

If you sell CDs and merchandise yourself, the only real advantage is that you get to keep all the profits. But it also means you'll be responsible for handling all the dirty work. For starters, you'll need to set up a secure method for accepting online payments. Setting yourself up to accept credit cards is an option, but credit-card companies charge a lot for the privilege of being a vendor—you'll likely find that you're not selling enough to justify the expense. There are companies that facilitate online payments. PayPal is probably the most trusted and recognized e-commerce name providing this service for small businesses, but they'll all charge you a small percentage for each transaction. Keep in mind that you'll need to fulfill all of the orders, which entails corresponding with each person when they order and when the package ships, as well as licking stamps, stuffing boxes, and hauling all that crap to the post office.

My recommendation would be to sign up with a third-party partner for your e-commerce needs and provide a link that takes users directly to your page on their site. They'll take care of the dirty work for the most part (although some only take the orders and require you to handle shipping), but they'll charge you a small fee for the service. The upside, though, is that they receive far more traffic in a day than your site will see in a month, and if they use collaborative filtering ("people who bought the CD by Band A also like…") to sell CDs, you're likely to sell more product and gain a few new fans without having to lift a finger.

Some third-party companies only sell CDs, while others sell anything you want to send to them. Among the best and most popular e-commerce sites for independent musicians are *www.cdbaby.com, www.mp3.com, www.ampcase.com,* and Amazon's Advantage for Music program. (Other third-party retailers include *www.airmusic.com, www.bandthings.com, www.branders.com, www.cafepress.com, www.cdstreet.com, www.earbuzz.com, www.hostbaby.com, www.localsonline.com www.mixonic.com, www.muzictone.com,* and *www.theorangespot.com.*)

You might recall earlier in the book when I discussed UPC codes. Well, once you start contemplating e-commerce it's time to decide whether it's worth it to buy your own, pay a small one-time fee to use someone else's (a third-party retailer like CD Baby, for instance), or bypass it altogether. Having a UPC code allows Soundscan to track the sales of your CDs, which may or may not matter to you. More importantly, some retailers actually won't sell your product unless it has its own UPC code. You have to weigh the cost benefit yourself—UPC codes are useful, but they aren't cheap, and you could surely use that money on other things.

For more information on selling your CDs, visit any of the third-party e-commerce sites I mentioned above or refer to Christopher Knab's great summary of the most popular third-party e-commerce partners at *www.musicbizacademy.com/knab/articles/sellonline1.htm.*

Links

If you want to give your Website a little personality, you might consider adding a "Things We Like" or similarly-named section that provides links to things you are interested in. This might include links to other bands, artists, or anything else that strikes your fancy. If you're in contact with bands that are similar to yours it might make sense to exchange links with them directly to cross-pollinate each other's fan base.

There are numerous link exchange Websites, such as Indie Link Exchange *(www.indielinkexchange.com/ile)* that you can use if you haven't established contact with other bands. But don't go overboard with links, banners, or sponsorships. Some people believe that providing as many links as possible increases your chances of being discovered, but it just makes you look tacky and desperate. Be selective, and only associate yourself with bands, sites, and causes you believe in. The links you provide on your site say a lot about you and will inform how visitors perceive you.

Don't Over Indulge: Blogs and Forums

I happen to think Web logs (a.k.a. "blogs") are way too self-indulgent for band Websites. First of all, who cares what you did this morning? Don't make the assumption that people care as much about your minutiae as you do. Maybe I'm just crotchety, but I doubt whether anyone is interested in what you had for breakfast or how many bong hits your bassist can do. Aside from upcoming gigs and announcements about new records, nobody cares—no one—but if you believe your fans want to read a constantly updated archive of what you're thinking about, blog away…that is, if you can spare the time, oh self-absorbed one.

That advice goes for forums as well. It's great to think that people will want to talk to each other about how great you are, but you might want to wait to add that feature until you're sure you've got enough people visiting your site to warrant it. Think about it: When you're walking along the street looking for a restaurant to eat in, you're more likely to enter a restaurant that's packed instead of one that's empty. Wait until you're relatively sure you've got the fan base to justify an active bulletin board or forum. You don't want people to feel like losers for posting on a relatively inactive bulletin board.

BEFORE YOU UPLOAD YOUR WEBSITE

Once all of your pages have been created and are in working order, set about creating meta tags for each page. Meta tags are descriptive titles that search engines use to catalogue your site. Keywords ("instrumental art-rock"), site descriptions ("Fuller, an instro-cinematic rock trio hailing from New York City"), and other information is what essentially markets your site to people using search engines. Good keywords will help your site to appear higher in rankings on search engine results pages and will drive traffic to your site.

It's also imperative to run your Website through the wringer before you upload and send it out to the world. First of all, you've got to make sure that spelling and grammar are flawless. Then test the navigation to make sure it functions as someone who's new to the site would expect—no dead links, java script errors, delayed load times, or missing images to distract users from the intended experience.

Next, make sure to test your site on a variety of popular Internet browser platforms (like Internet Explorer, Netscape, Safari, and Mozilla Firefox) to make sure everything functions correctly. You'll have to make a decision on what an acceptable load time is for your users, but broadband usage is growing exponentially, so you shouldn't worry too much about dial-up users from the Land of the Lost, unless they form your core audience.

AFTER YOUR SITE HAS LAUNCHED

Once you've uploaded your site and seen it on line with your own eyes, set about submitting your URL to as many search engines and other music-related sites as you can. Start with the open directory *www.dmoz.org* search engine, then follow through with commercial search engines like *www.google.com, www.yahoo.com, www.altavista.com,* and *www.msn.com.* If you get your site listed with portals and online communities related to your genre, you'll get yourself onto the search engines through the back door. Either way, this will usher potential fans to your site when they're surfing the Web.

It may sound like an obvious point, but you should really try to get involved with portals and online communities that focus on your style of music. Websites like *www.jambase.com,* for example, can serve as excellent secondary outposts for your band and will drive lots of traffic to your site if you get yourself involved in their community. Lots of small bands find themselves in a position to promote themselves to hundreds of thousands of people simply by being listed alphabetically on a genre fan site. It's another opportunity to be recognized.

Andy Gadiel, founder and CEO of *www.jambase.com,* says his site and others like it help bands get discovered on line through simple association. "Our site is designed as a tour date search engine for fans, but we built it to allow bands to add their own information," he says. "This keeps people coming back and makes them feel that it's their site, their forum.

"More bands need to realize how many free opportunities like this are out there and available," says Gadiel. "We draw fans who like a certain type of music, and we know their tastes. When you become a part of this community, fans find out about you. Our site gives fans every opportunity to find out about the newest, latest, and greatest bands out there, and it gives bands the opportunity to reach these fans."

Once your site is up and running, mention it as often as possible. Use it in your e-mail signature when you send out any e-mail, even if it's not to someone who's into your band (excluding work contacts on the job, unless it's cool with your boss). Make sure you list the URL on your CD artwork, band merchandise, and business cards. And it goes without saying: Mention it once or twice during a set to let people know where they can buy your music.

chapter eight

RADIO AIRPLAY

I missed the boat. Commercial radio was apparently way cool back in the Sixties, but I was still too young to be aware of it. Only now, when I read about it or talk to people who were listening back then, do I get a sense of what was and what will never be again.

Back then, commercial rock stations played whatever they wanted. Sure, some stations had rigid formats (although not by today's standards), but the rock stations with nuts played whatever they were in the mood to hear, and it worked. DJs actually turned people on to new music, playing them on air before they'd even listened to the music themselves. Can you imagine that? One minute you'd hear Jimi Hendrix or Tiny Tim; the next it'd be some Prokofiev; Moby Grape; or Peter, Paul, and Mary. Back then commercial radio actually embraced the "anything goes" aesthetic. They weren't afraid to take chances, and because of that approach, people heard some incredible music that otherwise wouldn't have ever seen the light of day.

Jump to today and people are busy bitching about how no one's making music the way they used to, but that's simply not true. People didn't stop making good music—commercial radio just stopped playing it. These days you can zip across the heart of the dial and hear nothing but the same insipid song over and over. The genres might have different names, but the methodical, robotic, lifeless formats are exactly the same: Generic, homogenized, milquetoast.

Whether you're listening to rock, rap, or country, commercial radio is exactly what it says it is: Totally commercial. The computer-generated playlists cycle through the same one hundred or so songs every day across a syndicated network. The DJs don't touch records, have absolutely no input regarding the music being played, and offer no insight or knowledge about it other than what they read off a press release; they don't tell any meaningful stories about it because they're totally detached and, one would have to assume, uninterested in looking for the human interest in any of it. Commercial radio is nothing but a monotonous crap trap that's there to justify the insidious, insulting, overbearing commercials that bore into your brain like a drill. It's too much to bear.

Luckily there are still choices. I was fortunate in that I grew up near New York City back when commercial radio was still reasonably listenable and a number of college radio stations in the area simply kicked ass. I was hearing the classics like the Stones, Zeppelin, and the Who, along with the Pretenders, the Police, the Clash, Squeeze, Elvis Costello, Joe Jackson, U2, R.E.M., Aztec Camera, the Smiths, the Replacements, and a cast of middling fringe bands that were breaking onto the scene from the late-Seventies on through the mid-Eighties.

This doesn't sound remarkable today, now that all these acts are on reunion tours and oldies stations, but back then it was remarkable. These were my formative music years, and radio was a dear companion. But by the time the Nineties rolled around, commercial radio was a rotten carcass. Today's commercial radio makes what we were listening to ten years ago sound blissful; that's how much it sucks.

Thankfully college and community radio stations were there to save me. My access to indie music became more difficult when commercial radio's tastemaker credibility finally evaporated, but I knew those bizarre, low-watt stations were there down at the end of the dial where the radio ran out of numbers. I'd pull into my parent's driveway late at night and sit in the car with the engine off, straining to listen through clouds of static to hear my favorite college stations. That's how I stayed involved and attuned to what was going on in music. That was the source of the music that influences what I write and play today, and that's how I found out about new acts to see live when I was finally admitted into clubs.

While college and community stations still reside in the shadows of the huge monolithic radio syndicates like Clear Channel, they are the only radio outlets supporting the vital music you're making today. They're the ones taking chances on acts they like. They're the ones inviting touring acts into the studio for interviews and live performances. They're the ones turning people onto great music being made today and the great music that was made in decades past. They're the ones you should be dealing with if you want to make headway over the airwaves. If you're thinking about approaching commercial radio stations to promote your music, forget it. They don't even know you exist, and you're better off that way because if they had a use for you, you'd already have been exploited and left to die on the side of the road. College and community radio are out there right now waiting to hear from you. What are you waiting for?

LEFT OF THE DIAL

Unlike commercial radio stations, which focus rigidly on specific, yet vanilla genres and refuse to look at anything beyond, college and community radio stations cast a broad net and play all sorts of music. They won't necessarily play *anything,* but they're way more open to giving something from an unknown act a spin on the air just because they think it deserves to be heard.

On college and community stations, you're not going to hear the same songs over and over again, which is unfortunate if you're hoping to get played on the same station every day, but that also means there are more opportunities for bands to get heard. That's great whether you're looking to promote your music in advance of a tour or simply looking to pick up fans through on-air spins, interviews, and in-studio performances.

Bands can definitely benefit from this open-minded approach, but you've got to get your full press kit to the stations for this to happen. Unless you've got a distribution deal set up to sell your records and/or are preparing for a long nationwide tour, I'd recommend starting with stations in your immediate area, particularly those that support the type of music you play, and then hitting ones on the edge of your geographic region. You want to get airplay especially before you're coming into a new town for a gig, not the other way around. Be strategic about it.

TUNING IN

Start by putting together a list of all the stations in your broadcast area that play music like yours. Hopefully you've already got a pretty good sense of the stations out there and the ones that are appropriate, but if not you can sift through a list of stations in your area by visiting *www.radio-locator.com* or *www.gumbopages. com/ other-radio.html.* Do the same for Internet radio sites, which can be found by visiting *http://dir.yahoo.com/Entertainment/Music/Internet_Broadcasts/* or *www. bandradio.com/dir/Internet_Radio/,* but if you can't be bothered to select from a list, check out *www.fast.fm, shoutcast.com,* or *planetradio.net* to get an idea of what's out there.

Once you've got the call letters for the stations you want to reach out to, visit their Websites and see if any of the DJs log playlists on line. If they do that's a good sign that they're really engaged in what they're doing, and you should be able to tell based on the band names you're reading whether or not you'd fit in on their show. Many stations post these lists and let you search on specific keywords—like your band's name—to see how many times you've appeared, which is cool once you've gotten some spins.

You also want to look at their charts to see what bands are receiving the most airplay. Many stations post their charts, and some even send them to labels and the media, which can help you get noticed if you're flying up the charts on a bullet or consistently located at the top. That said, don't get caught up thinking what the charts say about specific rankings is gospel. No one would go on record to say the chart system is wholly corrupt, but many charts are notoriously inaccurate in terms of the actual rankings of bands. You can still get a good idea of what bands are receiving airplay this way, and based on that information you can eliminate stations whose programming in general doesn't favor your genre.

Make sure you know the names of the station personnel you should reach out to, and send them—especially the station's program director—your full press kit along with a personalized note explaining who you are and why you think you'd fit in. Failing to do this isn't a crime, but if you simply send it to the station, you're forcing an extra step in the filtering process, and that could slow down your music from getting to the person you intended.

"You don't want to send music to a DJ who doesn't play your kind of music," says Joan Hathaway, a DJ at WMBR (88.1 FM), which broadcasts from MIT's campus in Cambridge, Mass. "I'll pass packages to one of the other DJs if it should've been sent to them, but you really should know the taste of the person you're sending stuff to. We cross-pollinate and pass things on to each other, but there's no guarantee that it'll get played."

Packages that aren't sent directly to the programming director (PD) or a specific DJ at WMBR pass through one of twelve "genre" directors who listen, catalogue, and make notes about the records that would be appropriate for each show before filing the CDs in the station's library. The DJs will eventually read the notes that get sent to them by the PD, and if they have time they'll listen to the recommended CDs and play the ones they like.

Keep in mind that college and community stations have varying degrees of organization, time, and focus that they can spend on researching new music, but they receive tons of it and try to deal with it in an orderly fashion. Some have lots of volunteers working part time, others are hard pressed to get things done, but they take their music and the service they provide very seriously. It's ultimately worth the effort and the postage to send your package in to a PD, DJ, or to the station in general because it will eventually get listened to. These stations exist to educate and entertain their audience with music that otherwise wouldn't get played, so you've got a better chance with them than anywhere else.

Most stations receive enough CDs in the mail per week to not really notice when relative unknowns try to capture their interest with a novelty package. "In general we don't give extra attention to anything that comes with a fancy press kit, folder, bottle of motor oil, or box of chocolates, and generally I don't really give any attention to people who lobby via telephone for their play," says music/program director Brian Turner of WFMU (99.1 FM) in Jersey City, New Jersey. "We just look out for interesting music regardless of how it's presented to us.

"I will make contact if what they've sent is interesting, and I want to find out how to get other releases by them," he adds. If bands do follow up, Turner tries to let them know the status of their submission (pass, added, or currently in review), and anything he enters into the station's library receives related info in a database, so even if the disc winds up getting one play, the band that submitted it will see it noted on the playlist.

WMBR's Hathaway receives at least one hundred CDs directly from bands per week, ranging from small independent bands to those on small labels, and generally speaking she'll play anything she thinks deserves airtime. "If I like how something sounds, I'll immediately want to hear more of it," she says. "I'll play it once on-air, but then I struggle with it—there's something to be said about playing it over and over so that people get to know it, but if I do that, there's other music I can't play."

John Schaefer, host of the eclectic "New Sounds" show on New York's public radio WNYC (93.9 FM), says that it's critical for bands to acknowledge how busy people at radio stations are and advises bands to do their research before they start sending out materials blindly. "The best way to get music to me is also the least intrusive on my time and therefore the most efficient: An e-mail saying what it is and that it is coming, simply an informational e-mail, not one that requires a response," he says. "And then send a follow-up package with the actual music."

What actually gets listened to sometimes is a matter of luck, he admits. "Music from someone who demonstrates a working knowledge of the show, and the sorts of things I might be looking for, will usually get listened to first. Sometimes people will even suggest tracks to start with, which is helpful because if they know the show, it'll often get me to the most likely tracks on the disc. If they don't know the show, I'll get a good idea very quickly what kind of stuff this is."

Some artists view community and college radio as their first step in a progression toward an escalating fame, and for some bands it actually is, but to really attain a respectful relationship with a type of radio station you feel affinity for or think can help you, don't approach them with an overt agenda or any expectations, says WFMU's Turner. "Music directors get besieged as much as your average A&R label guy, so be patient and generally just try to let the music speak for itself."

Know the Show

If you decide to suggest which songs you think the DJ should preview first, consider their normal playlist and use the bands they seem to focus on as your descriptive references. If you say "this track sounds like .38 Special on crystal meth" or "sounds like early Wilco," that's likely to give them a strong idea of what to expect, but if that's not their style they'll likely pass. Just make sure you cater your suggestions to the DJ's established taste.

"It's all about targeting," Hathaway explains. "If you send me something that says 'we sound like Motorhead meets Thin Lizzy,' that's great, but that's not my thing, and I'm not going to listen even if it's excellent. I will pass it on, though, so it's worth doing."

Understanding what type of program a DJ hosts is critical to the equation—you should be thinking about their audience and whether it meshes with the target audience you're trying to reach. "With a program that's simply described as 'new music' or 'eclectic,' you might imagine I get a lot of packages that people are simply taking a flyer on," says Schaefer. "We get lots of garage rock, straight-ahead jazz combos, New Age noodling, and extreme avant-garde modernist stuff, none of which fits on our show, even though we often play pieces that may refer to those styles. So it is first of all vitally important for a musician to know the program that will be getting the package, otherwise you're wasting your time and the programmer's, as well."

Knowing what music a specific DJ plays on their program is critical, but knowing *why* they play what they play is helpful too. If you're sensitive to the types of music the DJ typically plays and the topics they discuss on air, you should be able to figure out if there's an angle that you can work to interest them before they even hear your music.

"My own criteria for good music are flexible," says Schaefer. "I will play things I'm not sure are 'good' but might complement other things I've programmed and the audience might find interesting. And there is a lot of music I consider to be great that I won't play simply because it doesn't fit what I'm doing. In general, I'm trying to imagine the average listener: A person who may or may not have a wide range of music knowledge, but who is curious. If something sounds like it might pique that imaginary listener's curiosity—if it piques my own, for example—I'll play it."

It's equally important to make sure your CD's packaging includes essential information (album title, name of band, song titles, and contacts). "Given a choice between a homemade CD-R and a clearly professional package from a major label with the suggestion that the artist has some track record or pedigree, most DJs will opt for the latter," says Schaefer. "So if you're serious about your music, be serious about how you present it.

Make the package easy to handle, easy to read, and to the point."

That means you shouldn't send CDs in white-paper-and-cellophane CD envelopes, plain cardboard mailers, or even unlabelled slimline jewel boxes. Why? "If your music makes it past the first step and is listened to, the DJ is going to file it, and if your CD case is too thin and doesn't have your name on the spine, it will be filed and then forgotten," says Schaefer. "It's a little thing, but to a DJ facing a wall of CD spines in various colors and various point sizes of copy, it makes a difference.

Hathaway agrees: "I'm relatively tolerant and will listen no matter how ugly or lame the packaging is, but you can't forget the information on the spine. Doing that decreases your chances of airplay significantly. Forgetting it makes me take an extra step, and that's not something I want to do when I'm looking at a wall of CDs."

The One-Sheet

Although your press kit's bio was put together to tell your story in general, don't shy away from writing a special note (a.k.a., a one-sheet), to tell radio stations something in particular that might get them interested enough to pick up your CD and really give it consideration. "Don't underestimate the value of one-sheet text or even album notes," says Hathaway. "I think there's an opportunity lost there.

Your one-sheet is a single piece of paper with bulleted information that gives whoever is reading it the basic rundown of your band. Make sure it lists your contact information, where and when your gigs are, who you're playing with, when or if you're going on tour, who's in your band, if any members play with other bands or are involved in other projects, and a quick synopsis or description that pigeonholes you for the reader.

"Where's the info? If you put the music in context for me, it'll give me an idea on how to program it," she says. "If you let me know about the different ways the music can be used, there are more opportunities for it to get used. Don't let music speak for itself; that's lazy. Don't tell people what it sounds like. I can figure that out."

"I want to be knowledgeable about the music I play," explains Hathaway. "Discographical details, like who wrote the song, who's playing what instrument, or if there's a guest artist, are all very important. Tell me about the session, how you met. Give me some history if there's a genuine backstory there, or if there's something interesting about the release in particular to talk about. Enable DJs to make connections and draw people in. If there's an interesting, short story, or fun fact behind a piece of music, we can tell that to our audience, and that gets them to at least listen with a level of interest."

INDEPENDENT RADIO PROMOTERS

Sending these materials directly to program directors and DJs is just one way to get your music in front of them. At the same time you're researching radio stations, you should work your network to see if anyone you know is connected to someone in the industry. Unlike regular music fans who might refer to CD release Websites or music magazines to find out about upcoming records, programming directors and DJs often rely on their own network of industry insiders—publicists, managers, and distribution folks—to inform them about what's coming out, and if you can somehow tap into those relationships, they might be able to help you leap to the top of the listening pile in a hurry.

After the PD, radio promoters seem to have the most influence regarding what gets played at stations, and since your chances of actually getting to speak to a PD are slim to none, you might consider working with a radio promotion company that specializes in college and community radio. There are roughly fifteen or so major companies of this nature, along with freelance individuals that handle all sorts of music, but most specialize in specific genres or formats. Team Clermont excels at promoting Brit-rock, The Syndicate is great with metal, Spectre is revered for how it handles hip-hop, and Planetary Group is awesome at AAA, so you'll have to do some careful shopping before you decide on the right ones to approach.

Radio promoters generally charge around $400 per week depending on your budget and needs. A typical promotional effort will last a minimum of four weeks and often more than six, so the cumulative cost can stretch your budget awfully thin. And even if you want to work with them, it's not that simple—they've actually got to decide that they want to work with you, too.

They'll listen to your music, and if they like it and feel that they can successfully promote it, they'll put together a proposal for you. They have relationships with all of the music directors, have a working knowledge of what stations play certain types of music, know how to get your music to the right people, and constantly call up to find out if your record is being played, and if so, how often.

Radio promotion companies might work with you even if you're unknown, but more often than not they don't because they don't want to waste your money and they don't want to be associated with projects that aren't going to be successful. After all, they rely on their reputations and word of mouth to bring in new radio clients.

Is It Worth It?

If you still want to take a chance and can find a company that wants to work with you, go for it, but keep in mind that you can do well at college radio and it still might not matter. There are different levels of popularity, and you have to know what you're going after before you sign up for a service you don't need. For a small band that simply wants a little status, radio promo companies represent a huge expense and a big risk. Wild success stories do happen a couple times a year for small, previously unknown bands, but when they do, no one—including the promotion company—can explain why.

If your band is truly prepared to tour aggressively and has a distribution deal, you can definitely benefit from the services radio promotion companies provide, but if you're not ready for that type of commitment it might be more cost effective for you to handle the radio promotion responsibilities yourself. Getting the same results as the pros is nearly impossible, but many of the promo companies do sell their contact lists for a much lower fee than if they were working your record, and that might enable you to contact the stations and do the dirty work yourself with a little more focus than if you did it all from scratch. Still, that data doesn't come with the expertise or relationships to encourage or deliver the results you seek.

"You can find phone numbers for stations on line, but you don't know what hours the program director keeps; I do," says Bill Benson, vice president of the radio department at the Atlanta-based, independent promotion company, Team Clermont. "Most program directors keep specific hours on certain days, and you could call asking for the music director and it might take you a few weeks just to find out their hours, and by then you're not getting the momentum of having a bunch of stations play your records at the same time. And besides, most music directors don't want to talk to individual bands. They like talking to us. They know who we represent, and they know us."

Before you leap into a relationship with a promotion company, remember that you've got to be able to pay their fee, and you've also got to have at least 500 copies of your finished, radio-ready CD with a booklet and tray card to give away. If you're not on tour and aren't selling your record through major brick-and-mortar stores, the only other viable reason to pursue a major promotion campaign would be to make a mark on the radio airplay charts, and unless you really think you'll land in the top ten across the country and thereby impress a major label, you're not spending your money wisely.

"College charts are just fake anyway," explains Benson. "When a major label radio promotion department calls a college radio station to find out where a certain band is on the charts, they're disappointed if their band, which they feel has top-ten potential, isn't as high as they had hoped. If the label person has a relationship with the person at the radio station, they'll ask them, 'Are you *sure* about that position? It'd be much better if they were higher on the chart…' and then miraculously that band is listed higher.

"When small bands get manipulated this way, it can be misleading," he says. "If you're hot on a certain station's chart but only two people show up when you play in that town, it's because the station didn't actually play you, and that doesn't help your cause. You don't need to be in a certain spot on the chart. You won't sell more records or get noticed by anyone by being in a certain position, and it won't bring more people to your shows. It's just a bragging right to put on your one-sheet."

Certain college stations in particular do have a huge effect on their listeners. KEXT in Seattle, KCRW in Santa Monica, and WRAS in Atlanta each broadcast to a huge audience, and if you can get played by them twenty times in a week you will pick up new fans, but if you're not on tour and those fans don't have an easy way to buy your record, they will forget about you in a hurry unless they're rabid. "Things are changing thanks to iTunes, CDBaby, and other online stores," says Benson. "It's getting easier now for bands without touring plans or distribution than it was five years ago, but focusing on big stations with the hope of 'making it' is a big risk."

Keep It Small

Instead, focus on the small stations in small cities and small college towns. Shoot for the tiny stations, not the big ones. You want spins on the ones whose listeners are usually the DJs, the record-store clerks, the coffeehouse barristas, and people working in the local clubs. There are literally hundreds of these small stations around the country where the listeners really get behind the music, and if they love what you do they'll all come see you when you roll into town. If you're good and they still like you after your first show, they'll all start playing it on the air, they'll all tell their friends, and there'll be a snowball effect. You'll come back to play that town again and there will be more people. That's all you can ask for.

Get yourself onto the airwaves. Strategize so that you can get radio stations to get behind your music and tell people who'd be interested to promote your upcoming shows in new areas as you expand your reach. They can deliver your music to an audience that's out there waiting to hear a band like yours. It's all about exposure. Use radio to attract new fans, use it to expand your market, and use it to champion your cause. But don't forget to let radio rock your world that first time you hear your own song come piping through the car stereo speakers. Roll down the windows, slow down to a crawl on Main Street, and turn it up.

chapter nine

SHOWTIME

Self-promotion can definitely feel like a thankless, even humiliating job, but all that tedium and grunt work pays off when you actually get to play your music in front of an enthusiastic live audience. Gigging is what it's all about. There's the focused practice and careful crafting of your set that tightens your songs just right, the workmanlike loading and unloading of gear, and the camaraderie that follows you from soundcheck to showtime. Then there's the heart-pounding adrenal rush as you step onstage, the ecstatic realization that the stage mix sounds great, the roar of the crowd that confirms what you're hearing onstage, and the knowing glances from your band mates as you recognize at once why you've traveled through hell together—your music sounds great—*this* is where you belong.

Enjoy your moments onstage. Playing your music in front of a receptive audience is a great thrill, and you can expect to be rewarded with many repeat performances if you prepare yourself to thrive onstage and use each gig as a stepping stone toward a bigger one down the line. Each gig is a part of a bigger process, and it's what you do along the way—how you carry yourself before, during, and after a gig—that determines whether or not you ultimately achieve the level of success you want for yourself.

The keys to success as a musician are writing good music, practicing it religiously, promoting your product creatively and methodically, and building up lore around your brand so that people are mesmerized when they hear your music and see it performed. The process for achieving this kind of success is slow and cumulative, inch by bloody inch, but if you bust your ass to play music that people love and figure out effective ways to keep them interested in it, you will undoubtedly taste success over and over again.

I'm not saying you shouldn't enjoy yourself at gigs, but you've got to make sure not to lose sight of what's important in the grand scheme. The hard work you go through to make records, build press kits, and book gigs has been done for one reason—to promote your music and achieve success—and that purpose shouldn't become subservient to your ego whenever your live show begins. The live show is just one part of the equation.

Approach each gig with the excitement you felt for your first one and the reverence you'd feel if it were your last. Do everything you can to promote it, go out of your way to capitalize on it, and always be in the moment so that you can enjoy and make the most of it.

BOOKING THE GIG

Whether you're planning on playing in one town until you've developed a following or you're planning on covering a larger geographic region to expand your fan base, you've got to pick out specific clubs that are conducive to your vibe and build up a reputation by playing them over and over and over again. Once you've succeeded on that level, you've got to move up in stature and start the process all over again. Problem is, booking gigs each step along the way sucks.

I blame it all on booking agents. They're the A.D.D. poster children, the moody masters of abject indifference and blasé rejection who can't be bothered to show up at work on time, can't handle the common courtesy of returning phone calls or e-mails, and can't give you a straight answer when you actually manage to catch them awake. Fact is, they'll make you so miserable at times it's hard not to think their sadistic behavior is reserved just for your band—until you talk to other bands and realize bookers are the same way with everyone.

There's only one way to win booking agents over, and that is with persistence. Don't be put off by their reputations for disdain and absentmindedness. Be positive, be firm, and let them know you want to play at their club. Contact them out of the blue and introduce yourself or just send your music and press kit (or at the very least your CD and bio) and then follow up in a week's time with a phone call or stop by the club to talk about it.

Don't be bashful or play it coy. E-mail them to let them know possible dates you can play. Always assume they're trying to book shows at least a month out from the day you're talking to them, probably two if it's a popular place in a decent-size city, and then give them some specific dates so that they can look at their calendar for a slot that will work.

If it feels like they want to give you the gig but aren't sure where you fit it, let them know what time slot will help you draw the biggest crowd. If you're having trouble getting a gig at a place you really want to play at, find out what other bands have played there recently and let the booker know you'd make a great opening act for them the next time they play. Dropping names helps, too, if there's someone in your band who's a known entity or if you know someone who plays there regularly who'd vouch for you.

You can't just drop off a CD, leave a message on an answering machine, and think that's enough. You've got to follow up. There's a fine line between persistence and annoyance, and you'll have to develop a feel for where that line is with each person. Plan on making mistakes and accept it as a cost of doing business. Use some discretion, be determined without being pushy, and do whatever you think is reasonable to get your foot in the door. If you still meet up with rejection, lick your wounds, move on to the next club, and start pushing your rock back up the hill.

"Following up is tricky," says Paolo Suarez, the booking/promotion associate at the Knitting Factory in New York. "You need to be persistent, but polite. It's weird. It often depends on how I'm feeling that day. You might be pestering me by e-mailing too frequently, but sometimes a date opens up and because you e-mailed me, you get it. Part of it is luck of the draw."

If a booker is contemplating a date for you but has never worked with you before, they'll inevitably ask you how many people you'll draw. As difficult as it is not to puff up the numbers, be honest. You want to develop a positive relationship with them so that you can play there more than once. If you tell them you'll draw 200 people and you end up only drawing twenty fans, they're not going to give you a headliner slot the next time you call. They probably won't take your call at all.

Even if you're being tentatively offered a plum gig and you know that telling the truth will blow it, tell the truth anyway—be forthright. Letting them know that you'll work hard to promote whatever show they give you will build more trust and good will down the road, and that's what you should be concerned about. Be realistic, clue them in about your expectations, and explain that you're building a fan base and that you're in it for the long run. If they like your music and see that you're consistently drawing more and more people over time, they'll be happy they stuck with you through the lean times. Don't worry—you'll eventually get the big gigs you passed on.

It's also really important to let the booker know that you can speak for the band when they finally come to their senses and offer you a show. Don't tell them, "Oh, I'm not sure. Let me get back to you." Be definitive. Make sure everyone in your band wants to play that venue before you start trying to book shows there, and make sure everyone in your group is available. Obviously in the course of life there are times when things come up and you need to request a different date, but the booker is not going to think you're playing hard to get if you turn them down the first time they offer you a slot. They'll think you're a flake, or that you don't have your act together.

KNOW BEFORE YOU GO

Make sure you know the venues you're booking yourself into, especially if you're trying to book yourself into a place out of town. A little research beforehand will go a long way toward making sure a questionable or unknown club is appropriate for your band. I'm not just talking about size of the stage or the PA. Find out what types of bands play there on a regular basis, or if bands ever play there.

You don't want to be pushing a pool table out of the way to set up or competing with TVs, the jukebox, and angry clientele when you start your first song. Basically, you don't need to put yourself in a dangerous position simply by showing up and provoking the natives. My first professional gig was in a biker bar. We showed up in our silk shirts thinking we were bad muthas only to feel like we had raw meat strapped to our backs at feeding time. Things reached a head when one of the patrons came up to me mid-song, gave me his best Altamont-psycho smile, and then pulled down his lower lip to show me the "fuck you" tattoo inside his nearly toothless mouth. I laughed nervously, he walked away, and we eventually won the place over, but damn, that was the wrong venue. There's no one to blame except yourself if you didn't do the leg work.

Information on venues is readily available on line, so you absolutely have no excuse to be clueless. Take a quick look at *www.pollstar.com, www.jambase.com,* or *www.matchgig.com* and make a note of the venues where bands like yours are scheduled to play. If you can't find a venue in your chosen region that's got a band like yours playing in the near future, go to *www.gigamerica,* which has an extensive venue database that's searchable by venue name, music style, and venue city/state. Other sites, like *www.musiciansatlas.com,* provide similar, if not more thorough resources, but you've got to pay for access. You should also read *How to Be Your Own Booking Agent (and Save 1000s of Dollars)* by Jeri Goldstein if you've never set up a tour before.

ON THE ROAD

When you're planning a tour, appropriate venues become harder and harder to find as you get farther outside major cities, so it helps to nail down gigs in your must-do cities first so that you have a general idea of where you're going and what those dates are. This lets you begin looking at secondary venues located between major cities and helps you plan an efficient tour. A map from a driving atlas will do the trick, but you'll be better off on sites like *www.mapquest.com* or *www.expedia.com,* which will generate driving directions between addresses that you provide.

Make sure to look for larger towns (particularly those home to colleges and universities) between the major cities on your route, and check them for known clubs on any of the sites I mentioned earlier. If you still come up empty-handed, you can try contacting independent record stores (www.the-ird.com/store.html) and bookstores (www.bookweb.org/members/browse.do, www.newpages.com/NPGuides/bookstores.htm) to see if they ever host in-store appearances. And if that falls through, check www.festivalfinder.com or any state's local tourism board Website to see if there are any festivals planned around the time you're coming through. You've got to do this well in advance, though, because festivals require a much longer lead time to schedule their performers.

Once you've got your itinerary planned, you'll need to set about finding places to sleep and eat. Yes, you can always stick with fast food and the trusty but rusty springs in your van's backseat, but you could also tap sites like www.deliverme.com, which finds places to eat and provides maps for virtually any town along your route, and www.couchexchange.org, which puts touring acts in touch with friendly locals who'll provide a comfortable floor or more.

PROMOTING THE GIG

Once you've nailed down the time and date for the gig, find out whether the venue will help you promote the show. Most clubs advertise in local papers, and many larger venues have a dedicated employee who deals specifically with publicity for upcoming shows. If the place you're playing offers this kind of assistance, find out what they're doing and take advantage of it. They might give you posters or flyers to hand out, or maybe you can redirect your efforts toward getting radio airplay if you know they're focusing on the press.

Even if all the venue says it'll do is put you in their newspaper ads and upcoming gig section of their Website, make sure they do it. No matter what, find out what their plan is before your show is set to occur, and ask to put up your own posters or flyers in the club a few days before your gig so that regular club goers know you're playing there.

Make all appropriate efforts to publicize the show yourself whether or not the club intends to help you. This includes printing and handing out flyers a week before the show, as well as dropping them off at the bar and in the bathrooms of other popular clubs and record stores to catch the attention of potential walk-in fans.

It's also a good idea to find out what other bands are sharing the bill and consider whether there's a good cross-promotion opportunity for you. Maybe it's worth teaming up to share costs for a paid advertisement, posters, or flyers. Consider ads in local papers and the free press, and if the papers' critics have "recommend gigs" sections, try giving the crits a call to see if they'd consider your show for inclusion. And if you've made contacts at local college and community radio stations, hit them up ASAP for some airplay or even an in-studio interview prior to your show.

There's a great radio station search engine located at *www.radio-locator.com* that enables you to find terrestrial and Internet radio stations by geographical location, call letters, or format, which you can use on line to develop leads. They also have radio station addresses and e-mail lists available, too, but you've got to pay for them—you should be able to find a mailing address, Website, or phone number on your own. In any case, try to send your press kit to as many of the relevant stations as possible and ask them to play your CD and hype your show as your pass through; let them know you're willing to stop by for an in-studio performance or interview, as well.

Before you hit the road, saturate local newspapers in the media markets you'll be visiting with your press kit, but don't forget to craft a specific press release about your upcoming tour as well. Check out Susan Glass' short article on how to write a press release *www.musicbizacademy.com/articles/pressrelease.htm*. She offers solid advice and even provides a fill-in-the-blank template that you can use to get started. E-mail the press release with enough lead time so that an editor can assign or write a story that'll appear before you show up to perform, and make a point of requesting a record review.

GETTING PAID

Your promotional machine is going to need fuel, so don't forget about asking the club you're playing how much money you're going to make. It may make you feel materialistic to discuss money with the club, but you should never forget that each gig is a business transaction. You're playing live music for the entertainment of people who pay money to see you perform. Those people pay money drinking at the bar while you're up there sweating through your spandex and leather pants. If the club is making money because you're playing music there, you should be compensated for your hard work and your drawing power. If you're a stickler for the business side of gigging, you will gain people's respect. Don't forget to take care of it, and don't let it kill your enthusiasm for making art.

Discussions about money should occur before the gig. Some bookers will try to make you feel as if you're being ungrateful by bringing it up, even though you're being totally professional. If you feel uncomfortable talking about it, try couching it under the guise of wanting to know what the bar expects before you play. Once they've established their expectations, that'll provide you with the Trojan horse you need to innocently ask what you'll get paid. Keep in mind it's a lot harder to demand more money once your gig is over. You've got to know how they do things while you're still in a position to negotiate.

Failing to talk about it upfront and then throwing a fit when you get handed $15 at the end of the night is a bad move. You don't want any surprises, like a ham-handed bouncer helping your equipment into your van by throwing it up the stairs. You especially don't want this to happen if you're from out of town—you need gas money to get back, and you shouldn't get stiffed based on someone's spontaneous decision about what to pay you. If it's going to be a flat fee, get someone to set a firm number. If it's a fee plus a percentage of the door and/or the bar, get an explanation of how the pay scale works and plan to have someone at the door to see how many people pay to see you.

It's always a good idea to have someone involved in your group at the door—or around it—checking in to see how many paying customers show up to see you. Hopefully the time will come when you're selling tickets to your shows, and you won't have to be bothered to see if the club you're playing at is being fair and honest, but until then have someone keeping an eye on the door. If you've got someone stationed to check how many paying customers turn up, give them an ink stamp with your band's name, logo, or URL on it; if the club stamps people's hands upon entering, this will be a nice touch, especially for the people who get too drunk at your gig and don't remember why they had such a good time the night before.

Contracts are solutions for solving the uncomfortable money issue, but it's hard to get agreements in writing unless you're playing in a pretty serious place. If you have your own standard contract (if not, *www.musiccontracts.com* is a good source), you can ask the club to fill in the blanks. You could also simply write your own basic needs and expectations on a cocktail napkin and get someone to sign it, but most musicians just wing it. I know I have, and while it usually works out, it's no fun to deal with the mystery at the end of the night.

The bottom line is that money talks, suckers walk. Don't be a sucker. Don't go on handshakes and what people say they'll do unless you've dealt with them before or aren't being offered an alternative. "Use your instincts," says Jay Rodriguez. "If you're getting a funny feeling about someone, you're probably right about it, so take actions to protect yourself." If it's a small gig that doesn't warrant the legal protection or some sort of agreement, you can bypass it, but if it's a big venue or someone's promising you a lot of money for a lot of work on your end, make sure it's on the up and up so there aren't any disputes later.

PREPARING FOR A GIG

There are a lot of things that bands don't consider once they've got a gig lined up because they're so happy to have it that everything else seems right with the world. Don't rest on your laurels. There's never a more important time to hone your presentation than in preparation for a gig.

For starters, every band should know what it looks like up on stage, particularly while it's in action. It's best to get someone with a video camera to record you from a stationary position, but if that's not possible it might help to rehearse in front of a mirror (many hourly rental studios have rooms with mirrors) so that you get an idea of what you look like. As musicians, we often concentrate so hard on our instruments that we lose sight of how we are standing or the drool pouring out of our mouths, but those physical facts are never lost on an audience. They're not conscious of it, but as they're watching you perform they are noticing how you carry yourself and it definitely registers.

By seeing yourself perform, you'll get a strong sense of what type of energy you are conveying. This is important because your mood will prove to be contagious to your audience, and even if you're feeling great inside, if you're standing around staring at your shoes when you play it's going to affect how the audience feels. I'm not saying you should hop around onstage like a madman if that's not your thing, but how you comport yourself will make an impression.

Most bands practice in the round, looking in toward the center at each other while they play, but when you get up on stage you're almost always facing out toward the audience. If you're not used to practicing this way it might throw off your visual cues and mess with how things feel and sound. You might sound and perform great in your rehearsal space this way, but it's a whole different ballgame when you're up on stage. You don't have to perform gymnastics up there, but the audience is watching your every move, and you really shouldn't have your back to them unless your name is Miles Davis. (It's not.)

One of the most seemingly innocuous but still contentious issues bands face is what to wear onstage. It seems like it shouldn't have much relevance in the context of playing music, but it's definitely worth a discussion to see how everyone thinks you look in the big picture. You'll probably find that some band members don't ever think about it while others are all worked up about it, and there are lots of valid arguments that can be made on either end of the scale. A cohesive look is always better than a confusing one. Unfortunately it's nearly impossible to enforce a strict uniform unless everyone agrees to it because it will inevitably make someone understandably uncomfortable or force at least one band member to rebel with an outfit so hideous their mother would hide. Handle these discussions delicately, then give me a call if you figure it out.

How you dress is a very personal thing, and one person's slick is another person's slouch. Bands on major labels are told by fashionista stylists what will look right—stripes on your sweatpants apparently make you taller, knit skull caps are still in for some reason, and bug-like Versace sunglasses are so "now"—and yet so many of people who take their advice come off looking like disingenuous idiots.

Having a unified look always gives a band an extra edge, but none of it matters if the music sucks. Beauty is in the eye of the beholder, so you've got to feel this one out on your own. But having said that, here are a few easy rules to follow: Don't wear your own band's T-shirt, don't get your haircut when you're drunk, don't wear shorts onstage unless you're shirtless and the gig is outside, and don't wear joke costumes unless you're afraid you'll be recognized.

CONFIRMING THE GIG

It's really easy to get caught up in preparation and promotion, but you shouldn't ever assume everything is on as scheduled just because that's how you left it when you initially booked the date. When you're a week away from your show, make a phone call to confirm that it's still on. It's even more important to follow up if you're playing an out-of-town show—there's no reason to drive three hours only to show up and find out the date got changed.

Give yourself and your fans enough time to change plans if need be. If you feel uncomfortable making the call or asking the question, pretend that you're calling to find out about load-in and soundcheck. If your time slot changed, you'll find out at this point, and that'll give you enough time to change your plans, call people up, send out e-mails, and revise details on your Website so that anyone who's interested knows about the change.

When you call to confirm the show, make sure to get detailed instructions on how to get there unless you're already familiar with the place—ask the booking agent, look at the club's Website, or find out the address and generate a map on line. Even if you're a macho man and don't need directions, make sure you have the bar's phone number before you leave for the show. Make sure that phone is at the bar rather than in some office that no one will be in when you call in lost.

If your band members are getting to the gig independently, make sure everyone knows the date, the name of the venue, the exact address, the load-in time, and the start time. And make sure you all leave with enough time to get lost or stuck in traffic and still make it to the show. Murphy's Law will strike when you least expect it.

It should go without saying that you should make sure your equipment is in working order before you go to any gig. That means amp inputs shouldn't be intermittent, every tuner and stompbox should have a fresh battery, guitars and basses should be intonated properly, the guitarist should have a second guitar or at least an extra set of strings on hand, and the drummer should have their stick bag, snare drum, cymbal bag, drum key, and special keychain bottle opener.

Don't forget to find out if there's a backline before you show up, and if there is one make sure to ask for a complete, working equipment list so that you know what crud you're going to get stuck playing through. Sometimes clubs insist that you use their gear, but if you're not happy with their gear or need your equipment don't hesitate to let them know. That said, if the backline is solid and isn't in bad shape, consider using it. It makes traveling to the gig easier, and the soundman will probably be familiar with how to make it sound its best in the room.

SETTING UP YOUR GEAR

If you decide not to use a backline, make sure your gear is appropriate for the stage or room you're playing. Small stages don't need big rigs, and large stages call for more than a practice amp. You don't want to show up with a weenie amp if you're playing a big hall, and you don't need an SVT if you're playing a coffeehouse. If the room turns out to be smaller than you expected, turn the amps toward the back wall so you don't blow out the audience's eardrums. Drummers who can't control their attack should throw a shirt over their snare drum or learn how to play with brushes.

Make sure you've checked with the club before you show up to find out the schedule for load-in and soundcheck. In more than twenty years of gigging I've never once showed up for load-in and found the soundman ready to do soundcheck, but I still keep showing up when I'm told. Call me stupid, but I think that's the professional thing to do, and I suggest you do the same. Plan to be on time, even if you've played the club before and know the soundman will be late. Fact is, if you're late to load-in and the soundperson is there on time, you may miss your soundcheck, and that'll impact how you sound when you go on. Set the tone for your relationship with the club and be on time no matter what. You might not get a gold star or cookies for it, but it's the right thing to do.

Once you've loaded your gear into the club and either set it up onstage or against a wall near the stage, introduce yourself to the manager, soundman, bartenders, and anyone else who carries some clout. If you don't talk to anyone else, make nice with the soundman no matter what. They are God once your set starts, and they have complete control of how you will sound unless they don't know what they're doing to begin with. Being rude, unreasonable, or annoying toward a malicious or vindictive soundman will doom your set. You wouldn't walk into the kitchen to tell the chef how to cook unless you were hoping for gobs of spit all over your entree, so don't do it here. If you have specific technical needs, tell the soundperson what they are, and try to be accommodating if they can't deliver exactly what you need. They have responsibilities and pressures, too, and if you work with them things will have a better chance of going smoothly.

When it's your turn for soundcheck, don't waste any time. Get up there, help the drummer set up, then turn your attention to your own gear while the drum mics are being placed. Drum sounds can be the bane of every gig. There's so much potential for feedback with all those open mics, and that can make for a very bad first song if you don't get it right during soundcheck.

Once the drums are set, the rest will fall into place quickly if there's time left. Don't sweat it if there isn't, getting sounds and levels for vocals and all the other instruments is easy during the first song. If there's time, make sure the vocals are crisp and natural sounding, and let the soundman know if you need reverb on it. If you can't hear the vocals well, turn all the other instruments down until you do. If you're not sure what things sound like, step off stage and walk out into the room while you're playing to hear what it sounds like. Worry about monitor mixes when you're actually playing—you can't tell what it'll sound like until the room is full.

Tune your instruments before you leave soundcheck, but make sure to tune them again when you go onstage to play. The temperature and humidity inside the club at showtime is likely to be different than it was an hour earlier, and when the air conditioner kicks in or the stage lights start blazing, everything is going to change. Left unchecked, you and your fans will likely get an unwelcome surprise when you start playing.

Once you're done with soundcheck, get your mailing list and whatever CDs and merchandise you're hoping to sell. Ask the manager where you can set up—they'll probably have a table you can use and might even get someone to sit there and take care of it for you if you don't have someone in your posse to handle it. Set up in a visible, designated site that people will pass by or be able to find easily when they're ready to spend some cash.

Although you can't play your mailing list onstage, it happens to be one of the key components that most bands overlook when they show up at a gig. Some bands don't bother bringing one, others are afraid to mention it because it seems pushy or awkward. Other times you don't want to talk about it because it deflates a "big rock moment." But if people like your music, they'll want to sign up and will want to know where you're playing next time. You owe it to yourself to let them know the mailing list exists. You don't have to go crazy talking about it—mention it once or twice from the stage during your gig, walk around with it when the gig is done, but you definitely have to nurture it. It's not going to grow on its own.

Once everything is set up, there's nothing to do but wait until it's show time. If you're the first band on, be ready at the appointed hour. If you have to wait until later in the night, go grab yourself a drink at the bar, or go talk to the doorman about who's on your guest list. In any case, try to relax, and make sure to greet your people as they show up—it'll make them feel good about showing up in the first place, and that never hurts.

ONCE THE GIG STARTS

Make sure you know what time you're supposed to take the stage, and when that time comes get up there without delay. There's always someone in the band who inevitably disappears outside for a cigarette or into the bathroom right before you're supposed to go on, so keep them on a short leash.

The only case where you should try to delay a prompt start is when you're the opening act and no one is in the house yet. In such cases, talk to the manager or the soundman about waiting a few minutes to see if more people show up. Most people who go out to see live music regularly expect gigs to start later than advertised and show up later as a result, so giving them a few minutes to straggle in through the door will make a difference. Other times no one's coming, and that's just the way it goes. Play your heart out for whoever is there.

The reason you want to get up onstage as quickly as possible is that you want to keep whoever is already at the club interested enough to stick around for your show. If you make people wait around too long, you give them the opportunity to finish their drink and move on. Instead, let the band before you get offstage and then get up there and get ready to play right away.

There's nothing cool or impressive about taking your sweet time getting onstage unless you're the headliner, and even then it's obnoxious if you take too long. If you're the clean-up act, get onstage and start playing in a hurry. You want to keep the crowd that's there, and people will likely stick around to see if you can keep the energy from the previous band going. Get onstage quickly, giving yourself enough time to set up and a few brief moments to get warmed up (with your volume off), and then let the soundman know you're ready.

Your first song should be a killer. First impressions last, so choose a song that's going to blow people away. Your mood will be contagious. If you're psyched the crowd will be too, if you're moping around the stage the crowd will sulk. People want to be entertained, so start with something riveting. Go for the jugular, get the place energized, and don't let out any slack until you're ready to slow things down.

The first few songs of your set will establish the pace and the energy for the show, so don't rush through them. It can be really difficult to combat all that adrenaline pumping through your veins, but it's important to play the songs at the tempo you normally rehearse them. Fact is, you're going to be playing harder at a gig than you normally would—it takes years, if not forever, to control your attack when you're playing live so that you don't press too hard and cramp up—and the natural inclination is to speed up. Don't let it happen. You'll flub your parts, change the nature of your songs, and make them harder to play and be heard.

Don't stop to talk to the crowd until you've gotten through the first two songs at the very least, and when you do talk, keep it brief and to the point. No one came to hear you talk. You want to build momentum and keep it going. Don't stop to admire yourself or milk the applause. People expect you to be good, and you should expect it, too. Don't be amazed by a good response. Be even better.

If possible, try to start each song while the crowd is still applauding the last one—it has the effect of ratcheting up the excitement and makes the crowd feel as if they can barely breath. Try not to let the volume or intensity of the applause drop off too much until you're already playing the next song in your set. Pausing to talk to someone offstage or to drink your beer early in the set is a momentum killer. It gives people a chance to settle in and shift their attention. Keep playing until you know you've got them roped—you'll feel it—and then keep them focused on you.

Your set should be sculpted to create a mood. Don't veer suddenly from mellow songs to bombastic rockers and then back to sedate love songs again. Keep the stylistic changes as subtle as possible. Sometimes it's impossible not to play divergent songs close together, so try to place a song that straddles the fence in between them rather than forcing bad segues together, which is the equivalent of throwing ice water on your audience. Assaulting them with a headbanger after you just played a tearjerker is too jarring and makes for a disjointed performance.

Plan your set list so that you get people's attention right away, and then take them on a continuous ride that changes naturally, not abruptly. Tempo changes are inevitable, and if you can't avoid one make sure to break up the uncomfortable shift by saying something into the mic. That's often all you need. Sets with too many sudden twists, turns, or bumps in the road are difficult to bear from the audience's perspective unless you're playing experimental music or are a progressive rock act. Don't test their patience. And try not to spontaneously improvise the set list by switching out one song for another—it upsets the dynamic of the set, always confuses someone in the band, and often explodes in your face—just stick to the plan. Trust your initial judgment.

You should always have someone associated with your band out in the audience to let you know how things are sounding. Maybe it's your manager, or one of your devoted fans, but whoever it is should be familiar with the way you typically sound so that they can let you or the soundman know if things aren't right.

Just because you sounded great during soundcheck is no guarantee that the mix won't sound awful once there's a crowd in the room. Experienced soundmen know how their room sounds once a crowd is in the room and will set your mix based on that beforehand, but if you don't have enough people in the room the high end might be piercing or the lows may boom. If this is the case, you need to change it. Don't be bashful about asking for changes.

Whatever the case may be, be straightforward and matter of fact when you ask the soundman to make the necessary adjustments for the floor mix or the stage mix. Calling them out over the mic if things sound bad is totally unprofessional and will only hurt your cause. Ask them to make the change in the quickest, kindest way possible, preferably with hand signals. And if that doesn't help, don't throw a fit or argue with other band members while you're onstage—you might be right to be angry, but the audience probably won't get it and will think you're behaving like a petulant child. Save it for later.

As you're moving through your set, pay attention to audience responses after songs, especially ones you haven't played before. This will help you get a sense of what worked well and what needs to be changed so that you don't make the same mistakes over and over. Keep your stage banter light, brief, and strategic. Have something planned to say in case someone breaks a string, otherwise avoid long monologues at all costs. You've probably got no more than forty minutes to play, and people didn't show up to hear you talk for half of that time.

Don't assume that everyone there knows your band's story—say who you are, tell them where you're from, mention if the next song is on a particular album that they can buy, let them know about your mailing list and where the merchandise table is so they can find it after the show, but always keep your comments brief. Save your acceptance speech for the Grammy Awards.

Keep playing until the soundman tells you your time is up, and when he drones those fateful words through the monitor make sure you end on a high energy moment that leaves the audience wanting more. Say your thanks, give props to band before you if they were good and their fans stayed, do the same for the band that's going on after you if they're the headliner and you want to get on their good side, then introduce your last song by name and nail it.

When you're done, don't linger onstage looking for a cheap, gratuitous encore. You're not a bunch of seagulls trolling for food scraps. If the crowd wants more they'll let you know it. Standing around waiting for your friends to stomp their feet so that you can play one more song is lame.

Earn a real encore; everyone knows when you deserve it. You'll receive them if you deliver a great performance. When people come to expect greatness from you and you deliver, you will never leave the stage, and your reputation will grow. An encore for anything less is plain out corny. You want people to talk about how good your band is. If your music is tight and you put on an exciting, interesting, sexy, or somehow dangerous performance, people will demand more now and expect it when they come to see you the next time.

If you planned on an encore and didn't get one, don't fret. You'll get a chance to play the songs you were saving at your next gig. There's no need to force the issue. This isn't the time to try out every song you've ever written. Your set shouldn't be any longer than forty-five minutes unless the crowd is going crazy and refuses to let you off the stage. And even then, if you don't feel like continuing, end it right there. That'll surely get people's attention.

You don't want to ever err by playing a song that's not ready for primetime. If you didn't feel confident enough about the song to add it to the set in the first place, it's not going to suddenly become good when you pull it out of your butt. Playing a song that you're not sure about is courting disaster. No one builds rockets once they're in the air. Wait. Be patient. Put in the work, and unleash the song you held back when you *know* it's hot.

If there's a band on after you, break down your gear right away and get it offstage; it's a common courtesy that many musicians should pay more attention to. It helps them get ready for their set, and it's how you'd want to be treated if you were the ones going up there. With your gear pushed off to the side, regroup for a couple minutes for a quick post-mortem, and then hang out with fans in the audience. Let people buy you beers. Listen to what people have to say. Encourage them to sign your mailing list. You could even grab the list and walk around the room with it so that anyone who's even remotely interested can sign up without having to move.

Once you've had your fill of the congratulatory hoopla, make sure to ask someone you trust for constructive criticism. Find out what rocked and what still needs work. Listen closely to what they say so that you can parse out their useful criticisms. And don't worry about inviting negativity. If you were great people won't be able to restrain themselves from telling you. Asking for constructive criticism and receiving nothing but praise is a good problem to have.

Before you load your gear out for the trek back home, make a point of thanking the soundman and the person who booked you. If they liked your act they'll let you know. And if they don't say anything, it doesn't mean anything. Just let them know you'll check back in to set up another gig.

If you don't get the response you expected, don't let it get to you. There's rarely anything personal implied by someone's lack of praise, and you shouldn't let it bend you all out of whack. You don't know what else went on behind the scenes at the club that evening, and it's too hard to tell how someone really feels based on their initial reaction or a lack thereof. And in any case, your success won't hinge on one gig. Don't get caught up with the concept of overnight success. Becoming successful is a slow process, and you should find some satisfaction with each little victory along the way.

Each new gig represents an opportunity to learn something new about yourself and your music. You don't have to have an out-of-body experience or some quasi-religious revelation onstage. All you have to do is remain open-minded. Many musicians get bogged down by past experiences and perceived failures and then they bring that baggage up onstage with them. You should try to treat each performance as an isolated, special event. You can rehash it when it's over so that you can put it in its proper context within the continuum of gigs you've played.

When it comes down to it, playing a gig is one of the most liberating experiences you can have. Whether there are thousands of people watching or only a handful shouldn't matter once you step onstage. You should go out there each time looking to enjoy yourself and entertain whoever is there.

Gigs don't have to be about how much money you make or the size of the audience (although those things definitely matter). Maybe one night you'll figure out how to become comfortable speaking into the mic in between songs while hundreds of people are staring at you. Perhaps you'll finally realize that your amps are too loud for the stage and that if you turned down you could perform better because the monitors wouldn't have to be cranked up to the point of feedback. Or maybe you'll figure out that your forearm is cramping up during the first few songs of the set because you're so excited you're overplaying.

Whatever the case may be, gigs aren't just about how many people show up or how loud the applause is. Each gig represents a fresh opportunity for you and your fans. Leave bad experiences from the past offstage so that they don't obstruct your freedom and restrict your musical spontaneity. When things don't go the way you want, move on. And when they do go right and everything is clicking—and that *will* happen more and more consistently if you stay the course—make sure to acknowledge the moment and be thankful for it. There's nothing better.

EPILOGUE

I t's a common saying among renowned artists that those who can, do; and those who can't, write about it. I happen to do both (rather well, I like to think), and being able to live both lives is what qualified me to write this type of book.

Sorry if that sounds cocky, but I take great pride in what I've accomplished here. Being a musician and a writer for a living is no easy feat. I've gained valuable experience in both areas. To some people that makes me a jack of all trades, master of none, but I'd argue that I'm very good at both, and getting better all the time. I'm a work in progress, and there's nothing wrong with progress.

Progress is success. Progress is the result of hard work and a continuous, unrelenting effort over time. In my case, I have worked hard to become a proficient musician, and I've worked equally hard to become a professional writer. While I haven't achieved everything I hope to in either pursuit, I've accomplished some things I'm very proud of. The dividends are real.

One of my most recent triumphs was completing this damn book. While I was writing it I loathed it, but as I sit here now mulling over these last few bits, I have forgotten all the miserable nights strung out over painstaking months of writing, and all I feel now is what one of my musical heroes, the great Paul Westerberg, might call a sense of "gratifaction."

The real achievement of starting and finishing a book, in my mind, is not typing the last word or cashing checks from the publisher—it's about what you learn along the way and what you do with that information. During the process of researching and writing this monster I was forced to reexamine how I go about my business, both as a musician and in general, and what I saw is worth sharing.

Humanity knows many scourges of the mind and body, but none affect artists more than procrastination; it is the disease of progress. Not all artists suffer with it, but many—most, including me—do. Doctors might call it attention deficit disorder; high school guidance counselors may call it a "slacker" attitude. Call it whatever you like, but procrastination is the enemy. It is what gets in between you and your great ideas, and if you don't learn to avoid it or manage it, you will suffer the consequences.

What are the consequences? Essentially it amounts to falling short of your goals. Procrastination always gets the best of you because when it strikes you are unable to give your best. Yeah, that sounds cheesy, but it's true: You really shouldn't be willing to accept anything from yourself but your best effort.

Procrastinators are essentially liars; well-intentioned liars, perhaps, but liars nonetheless. Mostly the lies are directed inward, but that's because we're the only ones who'd let it slide. That's what we do—we make excuses. Admittedly it's difficult to maintain a tenacious approach in every aspect of your art at all times, and there are times when you start to feel like you'll be able to do what you say, but the best intentions often go awry. Musicians in particular get so caught up focusing on the cool stuff like recording or gigging that we lose sight of the crap like making phone calls, writing letters, or passing out flyers. Generally speaking, we over-promise and under-deliver, and that's not the way you get ahead in any aspect of life.

It's not like being a procrastinator is a crime, but if you get lazy and let it creep into your approach to life, there's no telling the damage it can cause. The damage itself is invisible—it's only detectable by the absence of progress in areas where there should have been evidence to the contrary. Basically, there's no way to know what you might have achieved if you had wandered off the path of the righteous. That doesn't mean that you can't create great art as a procrastinator, but there's no way to know how much more prolific you might have been if you had a better work ethic.

Take me, for example: If I hadn't procrastinated while I wrote this book I could've finished it in two months rather than the year it took while I dragged my feet before finally writing it. Would it have been a better book if I had busted my ass up front? I don't know the answer to that, but it wouldn't have been worse, and it would have been *done,* leaving me more time to deal with other important activities that could've helped push my career along at a quicker pace.

Everybody, to some extent, procrastinates, but for whatever reason musicians are most notorious. I don't know why that is, I just know it's the case. That's why the rest of society sees us as slightly dysfunctional flakes. In my case, I always thought I thrived under pressure and could get a lot done in a hurry, but in retrospect my whole life has been one of doing just enough at the last minute to get the desired result rather than doing everything I possibly could right away to exceed my own expectations. In a nutshell, it's the whole "work not commensurate with ability" thing I saw on every report card I ever got in school. I accepted it rather than railing against it, and I've paid the price.

I'm not lacking creativity or talent—to the contrary, I'm far from a slouch. My problem is that I'm good enough to ignore what I need to do until the last possible minute because I know I can always get it done. It's why I don't know enough musical theory, it's why I'm always scrambling to set up gigs, it's why I always wait to intonate my bass until my band is actually recording. And while that approach hasn't really blown up in my face (yet), it hasn't helped me get ahead in any aspect of my music.

The irrefutable fact is I don't know what might have happened if I had been more proactive in past endeavors. Maybe I would have experienced all the same outcomes regardless of what I did or didn't do because that's just my destiny, but I don't really believe that. I think we all make our own luck through our own efforts, and you can never have too much of it. It is the one variable that is seemingly endowed at random. We each start out with an incalculable amount of it, and from there we can attract more or detract from it based on our actions and inactions. I believe that if I hadn't wasted time by ignoring the practical, tedious crap that's so critical to my musical career until the last possible minute, I could've been busy stacking gold records.

You've read this book, so you know where I stand. Now the question is really this: Where do *you* stand? Any musician who decides to become a success must make a deal with themselves that they can live with, and maybe it's time for you to reexamine the deal you made with yourself way back when to see if you're holding up your end of the bargain. There's no rule that says you can't change the rules. It's your deal—just be honest about the goals and the effort it's going to take to achieve them.

In my case the deal is to do everything I possibly can to progress from making music in anonymity to making music that people want to pay money to hear. I'm realistic about the possibilities, and I've chosen to make every effort I can to make my goals real up to the point where it interferes with the precariously balanced harmony I've already got. Your goal might be the same or different, but the deal is the same whether you're looking for fame, fortune, or a lost chord. No matter what you want from life, you've got to do what it takes to get there. Pay your dues, do the grunt work, and don't worry about how others are being rewarded for their efforts, no matter how unfair or unbelievable. Do what needs to be done, and do it now so that you're ready to answer the door when opportunity knocks. And go with the best of luck…

INDEX